Healing Through the Mass

Rev. Robert DeGrandis, S.S.J.

Other books
by Father Robert DeGrandis

The Power of Healing Prayer
Layperson's Manual for the Healing Ministry
Growing in Jesus
Introduction to the Healing Ministry
Introduction to the Catholic Charismatic Renewal
The Ten Commandments of Prayer
The Gift of Tongues
Spiritual Bookkeeping
Young Peoples' Forgiveness Prayer
Inner Healing Through the Stations of the Cross
Deliverance
To Forgive Is Divine
*Self-Image**
*Forgiveness and Inner Healing**

Spanish Translation: *Perdonar Y Sanidad Interior*

*Coauthored with Betty Tapscott

All scriptures from the Jerusalem Bible unless otherwise noted.

Printed in the United States of America

Acknowledgements

I want to thank all who have contributed to this book in any way.

My gratitude to the editor, Jessie Borrello of New Orleans, Louisiana, who rewrote a great deal of the material. She also wrote the chapter on the "Homily." My appreciation to Ken and Charlene Lawson of Gretna, Louisiana, who proofread the early manuscript and gave many valuable insights. Charlene wrote the chapter on "Our Father."

Thanks to all who have shared their spiritual journey, especially my sister, Dorothea DeGrandis Sudol, who has her own healing ministry. My appreciation to all my friends, too numerous to mention, who inspired me with their living of the Holy Mass day by day.

I wish to extend gratitude to Rose Payne of New Orleans, Louisiana; Mary Lozano of Fresno, California; and Jennifer Hieronymous of Mobile, Alabama, who helped to transcribe and edit the original manuscript from tape.

Gratitude also to Sr. Barbara Vaughn, O.S.B. of Birmingham, Alabama, for proofing the final manuscript.

The Author

Introduction

"During the meal Jesus took bread, blessed it, broke it, and gave it to his disciples. 'Take this and eat it,' he said, 'this is my body.' Then he took a cup, gave thanks, and gave it to them. 'All of you must drink from it,' he said, 'for this is my blood, the blood of the covenant, to be poured out in behalf of many for the forgiveness of sins' "
(Matthew 26:26-28 NAB).

The very heart of our Catholic Faith is the Sacrifice of the Mass. We come together to celebrate the Eucharist, the focal point, the center of our relationship with God. In the Mass the great mystery of the life, death and resurrection of Our Lord Jesus Christ is celebrated in a sacramental way. As Catholics we must come to the deep realization that the Mass is much more than we hitherto imagined, for the Mass is indeed a healing service. With this in mind I would like to share with you some of my own thoughts, appreciation and love of the Mass as a healing service.

The traditional Catholic teachings of the Eucharistic celebration as a banquet of the Lord and also as a sacrifice are familiar to many. As the Vatican Council states: "At the Last Supper, on the night he was betrayed, our

Savior instituted the eucharistic sacrifice of his Body and Blood. This he did in order to perpetuate the sacrifice of the Cross throughout the ages until he should come again, and so to entrust to his beloved Spouse, the Church, a memorial of his death and resurrection: a sacrament of love, a sign of unity, a bond of charity, a paschal banquet in which Christ is consumed, the mind is filled with grace, and a pledge of future glory is given to us." [1]

However, in more recent years there has been renewed interest given to the Mass as a healing service. Father Ted Dobson has written a book entitled *Say But the Word* which beautifully stresses the healing power of the Eucharist. In the beginning of his book he states that healing in the Mass has been part of our Catholic heritage. "But in the earliest Christian days, the Eucharist was seen as a Sacrament of healing and transformation, a rite that brought wholeness to the people who celebrated it. For example, St. Augustine in his greatest book, *The City of God*, as well as in his last book, *Revisions*, witnessed to the healing he had seen in his own church as a result of people receiving Eucharist." [2] Also Barbara Shlemon, R.N., has authored a pamphlet in which she, too, stresses the healing power of the Mass: "Each time we attend the celebration of Mass, we are at a healing service. As we approach the altar, we pray, 'Lord, I am not worthy to receive You, but only say the word and I shall be healed.' This is a prayer of confidence in the power of Jesus Christ to transform our physical, emotional and spiritual needs. If we truly believe that Jesus is present in the consecrated bread, then we should expect to obtain wholeness as we accept His body into ourselves." [3] It is also my hope that we develop a greater appreciation and understanding of the Eucharist as a healing service, healing for the body, mind and spirit of all.

For the last five years I have conducted many seminars for priests in various parts of the country. In my discussions with them, I have emphasized dimensions of the Holy Mass which are elements of a healing service. As the priest becomes aware of the healing aspects of the Eucharist, then he shares with others the same. Throughout the pages of this book I will discuss the essential parts of the Mass and illustrate a healing factor. Hopefully, an appreciation of healing within the Mass will be awakened within all who read these pages, an appreciation which will lead all to sharing what they have learned and experienced. As Catholics, when we grow in understanding and participation, focusing on the healing aspects of each part of the Mass, our receptivity to the healing power of Jesus abundantly present also increases. One medical doctor after hearing a discussion on the healing aspects of the Mass, shared with me that daily Mass took on new meaning for him after he realized that it was also a time for healing. May the same blessing be yours!

Contents

INTRODUCTORY RITES

CHAPTER 1

The Church as a Healing Place

"My house shall be called a house of prayer..."
(Matthew 21:13).

Our churches are healing places. Anthropological studies tell us that men of all faiths, all religions, have always had a sacred place. A place that was not ordinary, but above the ordinary. Indeed, if you look into ancient cities, towns or villages, there has always been one place that was the common gathering place — a place that belonged to everyone. For example, in Spanish cultures there was and still is the plaza with the cathedral centrally located. That was their gathering place, the sacred place where people congregated in communality to worship.

As we enter our sacred places of today, our churches, we can expect, and should expect, to experience healing. In the Old Testament we see God calling His people to a sacred place. "When King Solomon finished all the work on the Temple, he placed in the Temple storerooms all the things that his father David had dedicated to the Lord — the silver, gold, and other articles" (2 Chronicles 5:1 GNB). Beginning at verse 11 scripture tells us how the Covenant box was brought into the temple: "All the priests present, regardless of the group to which they belonged, had consecrated themselves. And all the Levite

1

musicians — Asaph, Herman, and Jeduthun, and the members of their clans — were wearing linen clothing. The Levites stood near the east side of the altar with cymbals and harps and with them were one hundred and twenty priests playing trumpets. The singers were accompanied in perfect harmony by trumpets, cymbals, and other instruments, as they praised the Lord singing: 'Praise the Lord, because he is good, and his love is eternal.' As the priests were leaving the Temple, it was suddenly filled with a cloud shining with the dazzling light of the Lord's presence, and they could not continue the service of worship" (2 Chronicles 5:11-14 GNB). The power of the Lord was so great they were overwhelmed! Today, as in days past, the Lord is present to His people in the sacred place, the Church. As we become aware of His presence, we enter to receive.

From time to time many of us have experienced being upset and agitated before walking into a church. As we entered the peaceful surroundings, we sensed the presence of the Lord and all of the tensions and anxieties seemingly disappeared. That same experience I have had many times, especially as I have entered the Church of the Immaculate Conception, the Jesuit Church on Baronne Street in New Orleans, Louisiana. I would go there for a short visit on a hot summer day. The coolness and quietness of the church spoke so powerfully of the Lord's waiting presence. In that church a quiet reverence is felt because, over the years, it has been a gathering place filled with people's vibrations of faith and love through prayer.

It is interesting to note that in some churches where people are very devout, you can walk in and sense the devoutness there. On the other hand, if you walk into other public places, such as an airport or office building, you may sometimes feel the anxiety and agitation as people are rushing around. As we enter into a church, we should be able to feel peace. A woman recently shared with me that as she was going through some difficult times in her life, the only peace she experienced was the daily hour she spent before the Blessed Sacrament. It was a healing place for her. I thought that was a very good point. In many ways we have failed as Catholics to call our people to this kind of deep, daily personal prayer. There is tremendous healing just being in church surrounded by His peace.

We want to begin with the idea the church is a place of healing. Walking into church can be healing. In some parishes where I have served, there were many people who would come fifteen, twenty, sometimes thirty minutes before Mass in order to pray. Their prayers, as I see it, created a healing atmosphere for all those who followed. For those whose lives permitted this practice, their intercessory prayer before Mass was beneficial — for themselves, for the congregation, for the priest.

In the above mentioned Old Testament quote from 2 Chronicles we have seen that where God was present, it was a holy and healing place. In those times the glory of the Lord descended upon the temple which contained only symbols of God's presence and did not contain the Eucharistic presence of the Lord as we now have. How much more should we experience the presence of God in our own churches today!

When we first enter into church we sign ourselves with holy water, which is blessed in the name of the Church to heal and expel demons. Water flowed from the side of Jesus on Calvary. We were baptized; we were regenerated with water. Therefore, let us bless ourselves, being mindful of what we are doing: "In the name of our Heavenly Father, the Father, in the name of Jesus, my brother, and in the name of love, the Holy Spirit." That gesture of our faith, in itself, can be healing. Let us become open to the healing power of the Lord! Be it done to us according to our faith (Matthew 9:29).

Conscious of the fact that the healing process has already begun, we begin the Mass proper. We are with the family of God. This is our family. We are members of the Body of Christ and we are related to the people with whom we pray. Within the next ten years we are going to see a greater development within the Church that we are spiritually related. It is just starting to evolve. Through international movements, such as, Cursillo, Charismatic Renewal, Marriage Encounter and parish oriented programs, i.e., Renewal Weekends and Renew, we are beginning to relate to each other both humanly and spiritually. Any separateness we have felt in the past will diminish. These programs encourage us to believe that we are indeed God's family. We are members of one another, the Body of Christ. We are a faith-filled people who gather together to pray in a sacred place — a healing place. "For where two or three are gathered in my name, there am I in the midst of them" (Matthew 18:20 RSV).

CHAPTER 2

Introductory Rite

*"In the name of the Father, and of the Son,
and of the Holy Spirit. Amen."*

The Mass begins with the sign of the cross, an expression of our faith that we are gathered in the name of the Trinity. In the name of the Father, our loving Father who is merciful, loves us and sent Jesus to redeem and to heal. "For God so loved the world that he gave his only son . . ." (John 3:16 RSV).

Let us reflect upon our relationship with the Father. Do we have a clear understanding of God as a loving Father? As a healing Father? I must confess publicly that after twenty-five years of Catholic education I still pretty well considered God as judge until the Spirit touched me. Then I began to see God more as a loving Father. As we reflect upon the healing aspect of the introductory rite, let us consider here our own relationship with Him. Do we truly see Him as loving? Perhaps during this very brief part of the Mass we could ask for healing of any negative attitudes which may have developed through the years toward God as a loving Father. Attitudes which express themselves today with such thoughts as, "God sends sickness," or "God wants me to have this problem." To the contrary, our Father is love. The Son is love. The Holy Spirit is love.

Jesus said, ". . . the works my Father has given to me to carry out, these same works of mine, testify that the Father has sent me" (John 5:36). What are these same works that Jesus was sent to carry out that witness to us of the Father's love? Peter in the New Testament speaks of these works at the house of Cornelius. He said, ". . . how God appointed Jesus of Nazareth with the Holy Spirit and with power; how he went about doing good and healing all that were oppressed by the devil, for God was with him" (Acts 10:38 RSV). Thus, the Father sent Jesus with the Holy Spirit to heal His people. We have a loving Father who wants to set us free in body, mind and spirit.

The Mass, as I have mentioned before, is a beautiful healing service of Jesus and in the beginning of Mass we acknowledge our Father by saying, "In the name of the Father." You may have come to Mass in disagreement with your marriage partner. I believe our heavenly Father wants to heal you. Also there may be deep fear for sins of your past life. I believe our heavenly Father wants to heal you. You may have come with an ache in your back which is killing you. I believe our Father wants to heal you physically because He is a loving Father who wants for us good things. "If you then who are evil, know how to give your children what is good, how much more will your Father in heaven give good things to those who ask him!" (Matthew 7:11).

Many times in the New Testament it is stated, "He healed them all." As we recall from scripture, there were on some occasions, as many as five thousand present! Here we might ask ourselves the question, "Did Jesus really do that? Did He really heal them all?" In the New Testament there is not one case where Jesus said, "Go home and suffer. That will make you a better person," or, "I will heal you next time when I come to Jerusalem." Jesus was always healing, always doing the work of the Father.

The following are scriptures which reflect the Father's healing love revealed through the works of Jesus:

Matthew 4:23: ". . . proclaiming the good news of the kingdom and cursing all kinds of diseases and sickness among the people."

Matthew 4:24: ". . . and those who were suffering from diseases and painful complaints of one kind or another, the possessed, epileptics, the paralyzed, were all brought to him, and he cured them."

Matthew 8:16: "He cast out the spirits with a word and cured all who were sick."

Matthew 9:35: ". . . proclaiming the Good News of the kingdom and curing all kinds of diseases and sickness."

Matthew 12:15: "Many followed him and he cured them all. . . ."

Matthew 14:14: ". . . he saw a large crowd; and he took pity on them and healed their sick."

Matthew 15:30: ". . . and large crowds came to him bringing the lame, the crippled, the blind, the dumb and many others; these they put down at his feet, and he cured them."

Matthew 19:2: "Large crowds followed him and he healed them there."

Matthew 21:14: "There were also blind and lame people who came to him in the Temple, and he cured them."

Mark 1:34: "The whole town came crowding around the door, and he cured many who were suffering from diseases of one kind or another. . . ."

Mark 3:10: "For he had cured so many that all who were afflicted in any way were crowding forward to touch him."

Mark 6:5: ". . . and he could work no miracles there, though he cured a few sick people by laying his hands on them."

Luke 4:40: "At sunset all those who had friends suffering from diseases of one kind or another brought them to him, and laying his hands on each he cured them."

Luke 6:19: "People tormented by unclean spirits were also cured, and everyone in the crowd was trying to touch him because power came out of him that cured them all."

Luke 9:11: ". . . and he cured those who were in need of healing."

Our Heavenly Father is a healing, blessing Father.

In every way He wants to heal us. When I mention healing I refer to healing of the whole man; body, mind and spirit. Man is a totality.

We have a loving Father who wants to heal hurts, guilt, fear, hatred, suicidal tendencies, compulsions, addictions, hearts, neuritis, bursitis, backaches and headaches. He wants us to bring all of our spiritual, psychological and physical needs to Him for healing.

Many people have an unconscious fear of God, believing that if you love the Lord and get too close to Him, He is going to make you suffer, that somehow your happiness will diminish, that He will make you do things unwillingly or impose a big cross on your back to carry. These thoughts perpetuate fear and are inconsistent with the idea of a loving Father. Of course, we would like to think, "I don't think that way," but we need to question ourselves to see if we do not carry these fears unconsciously. The opposite to these hidden fears is the Father's healing love. As we accept His love, our lives will grow in happiness and joy. This is the life-giving promise made to us through Jesus: "I have come that they may have life, and have it abundantly" (John 10:10 RSV). Also a big cross will not be imposed upon us as Jesus has carried the cross for us. If we do feel burdened, Jesus calls us, "Come to me, all who labor and are heavy laden, and I will give you rest" (Matthew 11:28). Such is the Father's love.

Primarily, these hidden fears grew out of a religious education that taught a theology of suffering, therefore many are still afraid of God and associate religion with suffering. Secondly, only secondly, do we remember reading in the lives of the saints how they experienced the closeness, the love, the warmth of the Father, Jesus Christ and the Holy Spirit. The cross was often accentuated without adverting to the great love which Jesus extends. In our society seemingly it is the norm to accentuate the negative instead of affirming the good. All of this affects our relationship with Jesus Christ and our Heavenly Father. Let us seek healing of these negative attitudes toward the Father and seek to receive His love.

Yes, God the Father sent Jesus in His name to show us His love — for Jesus to do good, to redeem and to heal. Throughout Jesus' ministry the Pharisees were waiting for Him to act contrary to the law of Moses. Jesus, however, knew of their deviousness and warned His followers in these words: "Remember, I am sending you out like sheep among wolves; so be cunning as serpents and yet as harmless as doves" (Matthew 10:16). When we consider the times, we have to believe that these sayings were easy, but the true test of the matter was difficult. An example of this can be found in Luke 6:6-11, when Jesus healed the man with the withered hand. The Pharisees, being strict practitioners of the law, saw this as a reproach on the law given to Moses and they questioned Jesus. Today the question remains, "Why would Jesus act contrary to the law?" It is as simple as this: love impels people to act in an imprudent manner. Jesus was filled with compassion for this man with the withered hand so it did not matter that it was the Sabbath. Imagine, if you will, that this man was a carpenter like Jesus. Imagine also that he could not work because of his hand. Jesus, being skilled in that trade, could understand the dilemma of being unable to use his hands to work. Therefore, impelled by love, rather than the law, He healed to the dismay and the rage of the Pharisees. Though the act may have been forceful, Jesus was perfect and His actions were not meant to bring division into the law but to fulfill the law (Matthew 5:17). Moreover, He wanted to show the people that the law was not an end in itself. The law is not the final word. God's love, His healing and redeeming love, is the final word.

In the name of the Father who sent Jesus to heal us; in the name of the Son, Jesus the healer, who tells His disciples to preach the Gospel and heal the sick (Mark 3:14); in the name of the Holy Spirit who empowers us to do the work of Jesus (John 20:12-23).

In the introductory rite as we sign ourselves with the sign of the cross, may we enter into a deeper appreciation of the Father's healing love, remembering God is love and as a loving Father He desires for us to receive and enter into His love. In closing, I quote a very short, but powerful, line from Peter van Breeman's book *As Bread That Is Broken:* "God cannot but love totally — 100%." [4] This is the way He loves — totally. Let us seek to be open to receive His love as we begin the Mass in His name.

The grace of our Lord Jesus Christ and the love of God and the fellowship of the Holy Spirit be with you all.

And also with you.

CHAPTER 3

Penitential Rite

"I confess to almighty God, and to you my brothers and sisters, that I have sinned through my own fault in my thoughts and in my words, in what I have done and in what I have failed to do; and I ask blessed Mary, ever virgin, all the angels and saints, and you, my brothers and sisters, to pray for me to the Lord our God.

"May almighty God have mercy on us, forgive us our sins, and bring us to everlasting life."

Forgiveness is primary in our healing process, therefore, I consider the Penitential Rite to be one of the most healing parts of the Mass. Firstly, healing centers around the fact that our Heavenly Father forgives us unconditionally. He forgives us, heals our wounds and welcomes us home (Luke 15:11-32). During the Mass as we gather for Eucharist, for thanksgiving, a celebration of forgiveness, let us remember it is only by an action of the Holy Spirit in our hearts and minds that will bring us to the point where we can say, "Yes, I really believe the Father forgives me for all the wrong I have done." As we open ourselves to God's Spirit moving in our hearts we are able to accept His love just as we are. Secondly, our attitudes of forgiveness are conditional. We are limited in our ability to forgive. To forgive completely is a divine action needing the help of Jesus. As we seek His help we will grow in receptivity to His forgiveness and acceptance, then our forgiveness and acceptance of others also increases. Can you forgive your mother-in-law who has caused difficulty in your family? Can you forgive your neighbors? This is why the Penitential Rite is so important; we are preparing our hearts, cleansing our hearts, to receive Jesus.

In the past I resented the fact that at the beginning of Mass, as we gathered as a Christian community, we immediately began to confess our sins. At that time it seemed to be a negative beginning. Now I realize that this part of the Mass is spiritually and psychologically the ideal place where we turn to the Lord and say, "Forgive me, Lord, as I forgive those who trespass against me." The Penitential Rite, I believe, is the key to healing through the Mass because it is here we open ourselves to receive the forgiveness of the Lord, and, more importantly, to reach out in forgiveness of one another and ourselves.

While riding on an airplane a number of years ago I read a magazine article dealing with a new psychiatry called family psychiatry. Instead of bringing in separately the son, daughter, mother or father for counseling, the whole family, even close friends, meet with the counsellor. Collectively the family members work on the tensions between them, enabling healing to come more quickly, deeper and better for the family as a whole. Exactly what does all this mean to us? Basically, in family psychiatry they are concentrating on the healing of relationships. It is believed that most psychological problems are caused by negative relationships within the family. After many years of new psychological approaches and techniques, psychology and psychiatry have become aligned, to some degree, with the scriptural approaches to healing of emotional illness — through forgiveness. Jesus tells us in scripture, "So then, if you are bringing your offering to the altar and there remember that your brother has something against you, leave your offering there before the altar, go and be reconciled with your brother first, and then come back and present your offering" (Matthew 5:23-24). Jesus' own emphasis on forgiveness explains why we have the Penitential Rite of the Mass at the beginning. Forgiveness received and given precedes the part of the Mass where we offer ourselves, our lives to the Lord.

After eighteen years in the healing ministry, I find it rewarding and stimulating to read books on holistic medicine with new healing approaches. As I watch for the areas where authors write about forgiveness, especially in interpersonal relationships. It is there that spiritual healing is touched upon.

When I was in Washington, D.C. a few years ago conducting a parish mission, there was a friend of mine in attendance. During that time he was taking classes in psychiatry. The following day when he returned to his classes, he mentioned my presence in his parish and that my prayer for healing contained many of the same aspects that had been previously covered in their lectures and discussions. They were talking about relationships and the need for forgiveness. Forgivensss is so important in the healing process that I always give it special, if not primary emphasis. I cannot emphasize it enough!

Of all the people I haved prayed with over the years, I would estimate that 90% have a need to forgive. Unforgiveness can block the arteries of life, the channels of love. Areas of unforgiveness, bitterness or resentment cause many types of problems: physical, psychological, emotional and spiritual. Forgiveness is the cleansing agent that unclogs our souls, freeing us to give and receive love.

Forgiveness is for everyone. Many people I meet say that they have no one to forgive. It has been my experience, however, we all need to extend forgiveness, especially focusing on self-forgiveness for sins of the past. We also need to forgive ourselves for any unconscious resentment that we might have toward God because of hurts, pains, death of a loved one or an unanswered prayer. Consciously, we realize that God is perfect and did not impose these burdens on us, however unconsciously we may carry resentment. Also another area in which there is ongoing forgiveness is with our father/mother relationships. Someone recently came to me and said, "You know, I didn't realize until today, when the Lord touched me, how much resentment I had toward my mother. All these years that I have been working with your ministry and in the inner healing ministry, it never occurred to me before as it did today how much I needed to forgive her." Always there is the need to forgive our father, mother, sisters, brothers, relatives and marriage partners. Also you may need to forgive your children. Invariably, parents think that their children do not give them enough love, affirmation and support. Also parents need to forgive their children for being out of fellowship with the Church. A woman said to me, "Father, until I heard you speak today I never realized that I have not forgiven my son who married a Mormon girl. He left the Catholic Church to become active in the Mormon Church. I realize now how much I resented that and have never forgiven him. It has upset me so much until I heard your talk today, and I forgave him." Also we need to forgive blood relatives. There is going to be interference in the family in some way and especially with in-laws.

Co-workers need to be forgiven for causing dissension in the office or on the job. In fact, people in management tell me that keeping peace among co-workers is one of their main and most difficult problems. Employers, employees, neighbors and church people need to be forgiven. We especially need to forgive the Church. I do not believe you can be reared in any religious institution and avoid being hurt. Within the Catholic Church we need to forgive bishops, priests, nuns, parish council members, superiors for hurts in the past and present.

THE VERY ESSENCE OF EFFECTIVE HEALING IS FORGIVENESS. We may need to forgive the professional people: doctors, nurses, lawyers, judges, teachers. We may need to forgive friends. Also the one person in life who has hurt you the most. Who is that one person? I would like to think that by the time you complete your study of the healing process here, you will know the name of the one person who has hurt you the most. If you cannot think of anyone, pray and ask the Holy Spirit to reveal that person to you by name. Then you can have that particular person isolated in your mind and make a decision to forgive. To consummate your decision, receive Holy Communion for that person the next time you attend Mass.

To open ourselves up to forgiveness we will say the Forgiveness Prayer. Strictly speaking the following prayer is not part of the Penitential Rite, however it has been my experience through the years that if we can set aside a time to say the Forgiveness Prayer outside of Mass proper, it can be very helpful in opening oneself to appropriate and to receive the forgiveness of God. Also during the eucharistic celebration we can focus on the one person or the one area of our lives in which we still experience discomfort or conflict during the Penitential Rite. Many will find this practice very healing and freeing.

Visualize Jesus with His hands on your head as He says, "I have come to liberate you today. Go deeply into the valley of forgiveness and be set free."

The Forgiveness Prayer

Lord Jesus, I ask today for the grace to forgive. Lord, I forgive You for the times death came into the family, sickness, financial difficulties or what I thought were punishments and people said that it was God's will. I then became rebellious and bitter. Today purify my heart and my mind, Lord Jesus.

Lord, I forgive myself for my delving into superstition, using Ouija boards, reading horoscopes, going to seances, using fortune telling, palm reading, wearing lucky charms. I reject all these superstitions and accept You as my Lord and Savior. Fill me with Your Holy Spirit.

Lord, I forgive my mother for the times she hurt me, resented me, was angry with me, punished me, preferred my brothers and sisters to me, told me I was dumb, ugly, stupid, the worst of the children, that I cost the family a lot of money, that I was unwanted, an accident, a mistake, or not what she expected.

I forgive my father for any non-support, lack of love, lack of affection, lack of attention, lack of companionship. I forgive him for his fighting, arguing, desertion, being away from home, divorcing my mother, or any running around, for his drinking, for his harsh criticism.

Lord, I forgive my brothers and sisters, those who rejected me, lied about me, hated me, resented me, competed for my parents' love, physically harmed me, were too severe on me, made my life unpleasant.

Lord, I forgive my marriage partner for lack of love, lack of attention, lack of communication, for faults, failings, weaknesses, or those other acts or words that hurt or disturbed me.

Lord, I forgive my children for their lack of respect, lack of obedience, lack of love, lack of warmth, lack of understanding, for their bad habits, falling away from the Church.

Lord, I forgive my blood relatives, grandmothers and grandfathers, uncles and aunts, others who may have interfered in our family, caused confusion, turned one parent against the other.

Lord, I forgive my in-laws, most especially my mother-in-law, also my father-in-law, sisters and brothers-in-law, and other relatives by marriage who have hurt me in any way.

Lord, I forgive my co-workers who are disagreeable, make life miserable, push their work off on me, gossip about me, won't cooperate with me, try to take my job.

My neighbors need to be forgiven, Lord, for their noise, late night parties, barking dogs that keep me awake, for their fighting and arguing, their gossiping.

Lord, I forgive all priests, all nuns, all bishops, my parish, parishes of the past, parish councils, all church agencies and the Roman Catholic Church for all their change, lack of support, pettiness, bad sermons, lack of friendliness, not affirming me as they should, not providing me with inspiration, not using me in a key position, not using me in a major capacity, for any hurts they have inflicted on me or my family, even in the distant past, I forgive them.

I forgive all professional people who have hurt me in any way: doctors, nurses, lawyers, judges, politicians and civil servants.

I forgive all service people: policemen, firemen, bus drivers, social workers, most especially automobile mechanics and television repairmen who may have ripped me off.

I forgive my employer for not paying me enough money, for not appreciating my work, for being unkind and unreasonable, angry, unfriendly, for not promoting me.

I forgive all school teachers and instructors of the past as well as of the present, Lord; those who insulted me, those who humiliated me, those who made fun of me, those who called me dumb or stupid, those who made me stay after school.

Lord, I forgive my friends who have let me down, lost contact with me, were not available when I needed help, borrowed money and did not return it.

Lord Jesus, I especially pray for the grace of forgiveness for that one person in my life who has hurt me the most, and I especially pray that I may forgive myself for hurting my parents, for getting drunk, using dope, for those sins against purity, bad books, bad movies, fornication, adultery, homosexuality, abortion, stealing, lying, cheating and defrauding.

Lord, I beg pardon of all these people for the hurts I have inflicted on them, especially my mother, father, children and marriage partner. I thank You, Lord, for the love that has come to me through them. Amen.

If you now feel better physically, psychologically or spiritually, then you have just experienced healing through forgiveness. You should feel lighter and more peaceful. If not, then I would recommend that you read this prayer daily, very slowly for nine days, a novena. Ask the Holy Spirit to guide you, opening your heart and mind, through the forgiveness process.

To Forgive Is Divine is a book I have written exclusively on forgiveness. You can never read too much on forgiveness. Anytime I find a book on forgiveness I will read it because I realize it is essential for healing. Reading on forgiveness will heighten our awareness of the need to forgive, the consciousness of forgiveness, because every day, all during the day, there are times when we do not receive the love, respect and affirmation we need. Therefore, I experience forgiveness as an ongoing occurrence in my own life. As long as we live we will experience hurt, however we can be set free through forgiveness.

To conclude this chapter, the Penitential Rite of the Mass calls us to forgive one another and it is at this point that I believe the Sign of Peace perfectly expresses what it should — the peace of Christ that will come to us if we attempt to forgive. Therefore, I say to you, "The peace of the Lord be with you."

CHAPTER 4

The Gloria

"Glory to God in the highest, and peace to His people on earth. Lord God, heavenly King, almighty God and Father, we worship You, we give You thanks, we praise You for Your glory. Lord Jesus Christ, only Son of the Father, Lord God, Lamb of God, You take away the sin of the world: have mercy on us; You are seated at the right hand of the Father, receive our prayer."

"And suddenly with the angel there was a great throng of the heavenly host, praising God and singing: 'Glory to God in the highest heaven, and peace to men who enjoy his favor' " (Luke 2:13-14). On the night of Jesus' birth, scripture tells us that the shepherds heard the angels singing praise to God. Their song of praise reminds us of the Gloria, as we know it today, in the celebration of the Mass. We continue and echo their praise in the Gloria for it is during this part of the Mass that we, too, lift up our hearts in praise, worship and thanksgiving to the Lord as we say, ". . . we worship You, we give You thanks, we praise You for Your Glory."

In the Gloria we enter into praise which is the praise of Jesus before the Father. His prayer becomes our prayer. Our prayer becomes His prayer. We join the earthly priesthood into the heavenly priesthood. The two become one in the Body of Christ. That is why praise is so powerful.

PRAISE! This is what we are called to do with our whole being. Worship and praise make Jesus the center of our lives. As we become praise-conscious people, praising and thanking the Lord for everything and everyone in our lives, we are, in effect, surrendering our lives to Him. We are forgetting about ourselves and concentrating on Him. What marvelous works the Lord can do in us and for us as we center on His goodness and love!

When we praise we are acknowledging the Lord as creator and His continuing, active involvement in our lives. He is the potter, we are the clay (Jeremiah 17:7). As we make this sacrifice of praise to the Lord for all things, we will become more open to healing of body, mind and spirit.

Always we need to seek ways in which we open our hearts more to the Lord. Praise is one way in which this openness is effected. In the previous chapter forgiveness was offered as a way to open our hearts to His healing love, now we speak of praise. Healing occurs as we focus our attention on the Lord, allowing Him to minister to us, to heal us. "Through him, let us offer God an unending sacrifice of praise, a verbal sacrifice that is offered every time we acknowledge his name" (Hebrews 13:15).

Paul says, ". . . and for all things give thanks to God. . ." (1 Thessalonians 5:18). Healing through praise comes when we are able to speak the name of the Lord, praising Him out loud — even when things go wrong. The average Catholic should be saying, "Praise You, Jesus," even when the washing machine breaks or if the main tube of the television burns out. Many would want to kick the TV or scream at it, but would find it difficult to say, "Praise You, Jesus." It is healing to be able to articulate the name of the Lord in praise when things go wrong, surrendering to Him the trials of the moment. Remember that "in everything God works for good with those who love him . . ." (Romans 8:28 RSV).

St. Augustine stated that God does not need praise — we need it. We need praise to open our hearts up to the Holy Spirit. However, as good Catholics we would prefer to go back to just petitioning. If we only petition in our prayer, then we become the center of our prayer instead of the Lord. It is our needs that we are bringing to the Lord, but when we praise God we are focusing totally on Jesus, making Jesus the center.

The prayer of praise, the Gloria, is fantastically healing because it also confirms what scripture teaches, ". . . give, and it will be given to you . . ." (Luke 6:38 RSV). Minister to the Lord and He will minister unto you. It is in giving praise that we receive healing. It is in dying to ourselves that we are born to eternal life. Therefore, praise at Mass is extremely powerful. Many people can receive healing at Sunday Mass by actively participating in the singing of songs and saying the prayers, such as the Gloria. There is healing in almost every Mass, I believe, because the elements of healing are present. People don't talk about it, but there is healing. As priests, we need to say the prayers distinctly and with enthusiasm knowing that people present are being touched by the Lord.

Some very powerful spiritual effects happen within the heart as we praise. Above all, it extols Jesus Christ as our Lord and Master. Secondly, it has been noticed that people are much more in "unity" while praising. There is a sense of "togetherness" when all are giving worship to the Lord. Again we are one in the Spirit, not divided; there is "oneness," not division; there is "unity," not separateness.

Scripture commands us to praise the Lord. The book of Psalms, whose main theme is praise, was inspired by the Holy Spirit. The last psalm sums up the Holy Spirit's message:

> "*Alleluia!*
> *Praise God in his Temple on earth,*
> *praise him in his temple in heaven,*
> *praise him for his mighty achievements,*
> *praise him for his transcendent greatness!*
> *Praise him with blasts of the trumpet,*
> *praise him with lyre and harp,*
> *praise him with drums and dancing,*
> *praise him with strings and reeds,*
> *praise him with clashing cymbals,*
> *praise him with clanging cymbals!*
> *Let everything that breathes praise Yahweh!*
> *Alleluia!*" (Psalm 150:1-6).

Let us join in on this unending hymn of praise.

During the Gloria we can rejoice together that Jesus is here, He is with us today. Internally we can affirm the Lord's presence by saying, "Yes, Lord, I believe You are here. I believe You love me, giving me life today. I thank You for that love, also that I can work, talk, breathe, enjoy myself. Thank You, Lord, for the gift of family and friends that love and support me. Thank You, Jesus, for the gift of Your Holy Spirit. We praise You. We bless You. We worship You." Praise Him from the depths of your heart. Entering into the spirit of praise there is going to be healing for us, because the focus is upon Jesus.

Our sacrifice of praise is made to the Lord as we give up the right to understand difficult circumstances in our lives. We are trusting the Lord when we praise Him. We are saying, "I do not understand all that is happening in my life, but I believe in Your love and I praise You." It is healing when we learn to trust the Lord with our whole hearts. Let us praise the Lord in the Gloria for His presence in our lives today! Let us worship and praise Him!

For You alone are the Holy One, You alone are the Lord, You alone are the Most High, Jesus Christ, with the Holy Spirit, in the glory of God the Father. Amen.

CHAPTER 5

The Oration

Let us pray.
"God our Father, we are gathered here to share
in the supper which Your only Son left to His
Church to reveal His love. He gave it to us when
He was about to die and commanded us to celebrate
it as the new and eternal sacrifice. We pray that
in this eucharist we may find the fullness of love
and life."
(Holy Thursday: Mass of the Lord's Supper.)

"Let us pray" is the invitation of the priest with the
community to enter into the opening prayer of the Mass,
the Oration. As the priest prays with arms extended, he
gathers or "collects" the prayers and needs of the congregation and presents them to the Lord. The priest
openly expresses, "Let us pray," in which he is saying,
"Let us share today the overflow of our prayer life, col-
lecting and presenting our prayers to God our Father."
There is power in community prayer before the Blessed
Sacrament, especially when the people present have
been praying during the week, and now collectively join
in prayer.

Individually I would like to ask, "Have you prayed
daily? Have you gone into your closet with Jesus Christ?

"And when you pray, go to your private room and, when you have shut the door, pray to your Father who is in that secret place, and your Father who sees all that is done in secret will reward you" (Matthew 6:6). Have you been with the Lord daily? Is this Mass an overflow of your relationship, of your communication, with the Lord?" If you have been in daily prayer then, during the Mass, you are giving more than you are receiving because you are giving of the overflow of the action of the Spirit received during daily prayer. If one is not in daily prayer one just soaks up and receives and has little to give. Ideally we come not only to receive, but to give.

One way the Mass is extended into our daily lives is through prayer time. There are three legs to prayer life. The first leg of the tripod is communal prayer, the prayer of the total community. An example of this would be the Mass itself or in prayer groups where our worship and praise is communal. It is the Body of Christ, the people of God, coming together to celebrate in unity and solidarity.

The second leg is small group prayer. In South Korea there is a church which has a membership of three hundred thousand people. The minister has revealed that the secret of his church is meeting in small groups during the week to pray, usually in someone's home. Do you have a sharing group? Do you meet with one, two, three, four or more people during the week, or do you meet with prayer partners? Is your life of prayer not only in the total community, but in the smaller community as well? That kind of smaller group personalization is needed. It is vitally important that we share with one another our Christian faith.

Of course, the third leg is private, individual prayer. We, as priests, ministers and teachers in the Church need to challenge people more openly in this area, calling people to deep personal prayer. Most of us watch the local and national news an hour each day. We allot that time to keeping up with the local and national events of the day. The challenge needs to be issued for everyone to make a commitment to daily prayer, allowing time during the day to be spent with the Lord. For my own information I sometimes ask Catholics, "What was on the Donahue Show yesterday? As The World Turns? Dynasty?" Repeatedly they know, "Oh, they talked about this and such and such happened." Sadly, are not our people filled with the happenings and things of the world? Again I ask this question: "Brother or sister, are you setting aside twenty minutes to be with the Lord or to read scripture?" "What? Do you think I am a religious fanatic or something?" Then I ask, "How many hours do you watch TV a day?" Many times the answers indicate to me it is a sad state of affairs that enough emphasis has not been placed on personal prayer. On the other hand it is always uplifting to hear of those who are in daily prayer, scripture reading and meditation. Each of us could commit at least twenty minutes a day to prayer, opening ourselves to listen to the Lord. Perhaps if you have trouble praying, you could begin by reading scripture and reflecting on what you have read. Bishop Fulton Sheen said the Church could be renewed if everyone would spend twenty minutes a day in mental prayer, which includes scripture reading and meditation time.

There is a story of a woman who had a retarded son eighteen years old. Her husband was very jealous of this son. One day she screamed out to the Lord because of the problems which were occurring within her household. Afterwards she began to get the sense that the Lord was calling her to spend quiet time with Him each day. She then set aside a quiet time each day to pray, to read scripture, to reflect on what she had read. Over a course of a few weeks she began to see changes in her family and finally the whole situation healed beautifully. Oftentimes you are going to be the intercessor in your home; you are going to be the pipeline, the channel, through which God's healing power flows through your family.

When people commit themselves to daily prayer they receive a great deal of healing. A woman once told me that at twenty-nine she thought she was going to lose her mind as she was going through an early menopause. All kinds of things were happening to her emotionally. She, too, felt the need at that time to go to church everyday for a holy hour. She said "You know, there is very little that cannot be healed in an hour before the Blessed Sacrament everyday." There is a lot of truth in what she says. Father Ralph D'Orio, the well-known healing priest, spends an extra holy hour everyday and it is there that he receives his power in the Lord.

This generation is seeking answers to the problems of life by going inside themselves. Many young people are making commitments to daily meditation exercised in a non-Christian way. These spiritual movements and cults are flourishing today. In our Catholic tradition, there are many seminars being given on "centering prayer" which is a prayer of contemplation, a prayer of quiet. We need to emphasize this kind of personal prayer in the home. It is difficult to think that Christians can resist the pagan atmosphere around them unless they indulge themselves in regular daily prayer.

Increasingly, doctors are telling their patients that they need time to be quiet and peaceful since there is a sharp rise in illnesses which are stress related. A daily holy hour is a way to come into more quietude of body, mind and spirit. "COULD YOU NOT WATCH WITH ME ONE HOUR?" (Matthew 26:40 RSV).

My experience as a priest over the years has proven to me that people of prayer are basically happier people and are more able to cope with the "hard knocks" of life. As Catholics, we need to realize the very serious obligation to become people of prayer. We have been blessed immeasurably in our faith with Jesus as Lord, the Eucharist, sacraments, scripture, Mary as Mother. Let us respond with a serious prayer life to these gifts of God. As Jesus said to the Samaritan woman, "If only you recognized God's gift . . ." (John 4:11 NAB).

Bishop Fulton Sheen made a promise on the day of his ordination that he would spend a continuous Holy Hour every day in the presence of our Lord in the Blessed Sacrament. He kept that promise throughout his life and encouraged priests to do likewise. Perhaps no other bishop in our modern time has had such a powerful influence on American Catholics as he has had. His works live on. I believe his power flowed from his daily prayer life. I, as a priest, feel the obligation to spend at least one hour in prayer daily with the Eucharistic Lord and have kept this commitment from the day I first entered the seminary. If I have had any influence on people, I would attribute it to the power of prayer in my life.

For a moment, through your imagination, take a flight of fancy with me into a situation where every Catholic spent an hour of prayer daily. What would be the effect of this upon Sunday Mass? I believe the Spirit would spark within us a deeper appreciation of the Mass and Mass would become exciting!

In one archdiocese recently the statistics were given to the Evangelization Committee for the people regularly attending Mass. The statistician stated that only 8% of people in this western diocese attended regularly. Perhaps the people in that 8% need to make a daily hour for the other 92%! That is what being a CONFIRMED CATHOLIC means, that we are witnesses and co-workers with Jesus for the redemption of the world.

Parents are decrying the culture of today and feel that their children are being led away from God and Christian practices. As parents there is a need to take a positive approach through prayer for the welfare of the children, especially if they do not regularly practice their faith. Very few people seem to take the obligation of intercession seriously. If we believe in prayer, then spending an hour daily praying for the family members would work miracles. "Ask, and it will be given to you; search, and you will find; knock, and the door will be opened to you" (Luke 11:9).

I have ministered to many dying persons and never have I heard anyone at that time say, "Father, I have wasted so much time praying and now that I am dying, I am sorry I spent so much time in prayer." The truth is you will never be sorry for the amount of time you commit to the Lord daily, not only at the time of your death, but right now.

The three legs of prayer are community, small group and personal. When the priest says, "Let us pray," we are sharing the overflow of our prayer life, having been with the Lord individually, in small groups and now as a total community. Let us indeed pray. There is fantastic power in the Body of Christ and there is healing for the entire body. Ask yourself if you have been faithful to the healing that is found in prayer, beginning with individual prayer.

When the priest says, "Let us pray," he is calling us

not only to prayer there at Mass, but in the entirety of our lives. He is saying, with arms opened, "Let us live a life of serious prayer." Pope Pius XII said that liturgical prayer nourishes private prayer, and private prayer nourishes liturgical prayer. That is so true.

As we hear the priest's invitation to pray, the priest is embracing all our needs, all our prayers, praying as Jesus Himself prays before the Father.

Grant this through our Lord Jesus Christ, Your Son, who lives and reigns with You and the Holy Spirit, one God, for ever and ever. Amen.

LITURGY OF THE WORD

CHAPTER 6

Scripture Readings — The Gospel

"All scripture is inspired by God and can profitably be used for teaching, for refuting error, for guiding people's lives and teaching them to be holy. This is how the man dedicated to God becomes fully equipped and ready for any good work" (1 Timothy 3:16-17).

"The word of God is something alive and active; it cuts like any double-edged sword but more finely; it can slip through the place where the soul is divided from the spirit, or joints from the marrow; it can judge the secret emotions and thoughts. No created thing can hide from him; everything is uncovered and open to the eyes of the one to whom we must give account of ourselves" (Hebrews 4:12-13).

In this chapter we will discuss the healing power of the Word of God, the living Word, which has the power to change and touch our lives with healing. The powerful effect that words and more particularly the Word of God has upon our lives is beautifully described in a book entitled *The Mass in Pictures.* "We know from experience that the spoken word is very powerful indeed. Words can bring us happiness or extreme dejection. Try for a moment to recall just one occasion in your life when perhaps you overheard someone criticize you or were on

the receiving end of a verbal lashing. The effect was probably devastating and it was an experience we all dreaded.
On the other hand, just one word of encouragement or
praise is all most of us need to face and overcome any
amount of hardship in our lives.

"The Jews believed that a word was far more than
just a sound emitted by the mouth. To the Jew a word
was so alive that it actually did things. Now just think
again about those critical words that were aimed in your
direction and you will begin to understand the Jewish
mind. Were they not like bullets which slowly wormed
their way into you and really upset you?

"When we remember this Jewish idea that words can
actually do things, a new way of looking at the Bible
opens up before us. We begin to see the Bible as a conversation between the Father and man. It is God who
begins the conversation and at His word creation springs
into being. God said, 'Let there be light,' and there was
light . . . God said, 'Let us make man in our image, in
the likeness of ourselves . . . and so it was.'

"Perhaps we can see now what we mean when we
say that God's word is creative. Every page of the Bible
adds to the splendor of this teaching by reminding us
that God is love. His words are the very opposite to those
bullet-type words which gradually destroy man. They are
words of love in which He gives Himself, shares His
secrets, and reveals Himself to those who listen.

"What, then, should our attitude be during the
Liturgy of the Word? We can sum it up by saying it
should be one of listening to and responding to what
God has to say to us in the Readings. That is why the
psalm which is sung or said after the first reading is so
important. We call it the Responsorial Psalm because
it is one way of responding to the Word of God." [5]

While I was pastor in Texas I would teach my parishoners what I am sharing with you now: "When you hear the Word of God at Sunday Mass, expect healing, expect that you will experience God's love, expect that God will move in your life to meet all your needs." I would also encourage them to share with me their experiences. As time went on I noticed people would call me on Sunday afternoons to say something like this: "Father, I came to Church so depressed this morning, but as I listened to the words of scripture I was really lifted. I felt released." Another woman from the same parish called to say, "Father, during the scripture readings today I felt as if I were being lifted out of the bench on a cloud." To me those experiences are the ordinary experiences of many because the Word of God is powerful, like a two-edged sword indicating the very presence of God. As Jesus said, "Man does not live on bread alone but on every word that comes from the mouth of God" (Matthew 4:4). Scripture will transform us, transform our minds. As Paul says, "Do not be conformed to this world but be transformed by the renewal of your mind . . ." (Romans 12:2 RSV).

When we come to Church it is a blessing to be attentive to the Word of the Lord. Again, when I was a pastor, we would have a scripture study on Thursday mornings, taking the readings of the Mass; we would read them and have time for personal reflection and sharing. This is a beautiful idea for Charismatics who are looking to begin small sharing groups. I also encourage priests to share the readings with a group of lay people, to get ideas for Sunday sermons from such sharings. By listening to the responses of the lay people, we, as priests, are able to reach the level where the majority of the people are. I deeply enjoyed my Thursday morning sharings. I found that lay people have insights stemming from years of Christian living in their vocation as single adults, as marriage partners and parents. Some of my priest friends tell me that preaching is difficult for them and I understand this, but as we open ourselves to sharing scripture with lay people, we will be enriched so very much and will have no difficulty findings ideas and examples to preach on Sunday. This has been supremely helpful in my ministry.

How do we distinguish between the "logos," the word, and "rhema" which is the inspired word? Logos is the scripture. We all read the same word, but to each of us certain words will quicken our spirit, words anointed for us by the Holy Spirit. That is rhema. Those words are going to minister life to you, a word customized to your heart. In reading words of scripture you might say, "Well, I have read that a hundred times and it still does not mean anything," and yet you might read it one time and say, "I understand. The Lord is really speaking to me." We know His word because we have heard it many times, but now we know that word in our hearts because it has become personal. To know in our hearts is rhema. It might be from John 5:8: "Get up, pick up your sleeping mat and walk." That might just touch your heart. You might have been having trouble with your legs and really feel the Lord saying that He will open your heart and you will have no trouble walking again. That is rhema, the Word anointed for your spirit in your particular circumstance at that particular time.

Oral Roberts tells his personal story. As a young man he was on his deathbed when he read one of the miracles of Jesus, was touched by that Word and said, "Lord, if You did it then, You can do it for me now." That was the beginning of his healing. His brother then took him to a healing service. Of course, today we know the extent of his powerful healing ministry. There is healing power in the Word of God. Jesus said, "If you make my Word your home you will indeed be my disciples, and you will learn the truth and the truth shall make you free" (John 8:31).

There is a line of scripture which transformed my way of thinking. It was John 10:10. When I was in the seminary, I was sitting on the stairs of a boathouse by the river. I was a lifeguard at that particular time, doing patrol duty at night. I flipped open my New Testament. I remember it was about 6:35 P.M. "I came that they may have life, and have it abundantly" (John 10:10 RSV). It was just like a lightning bolt out of heaven. The thought came to me, "Jesus wants me to be happy." That changed my whole attitude towards religion. From that time on I believed in my heart that religion is meant to be uplifting and joyful, not sad and blue. It is meant to be life-giving, communicating Jesus' life and happiness.

I recall another story of a young lady taking her final exams in nursing school. She was concerned about taking these tests and had been studying for three nights continuously. As she opened her Bible looking for words of encouragement, the words that spoke to her were, "Trust in the Lord with all your heart, on your own intelligence rely not . . ." (Proverbs 3:5 NAB). She still remembers to this day the impact those words had on her life. During her tests she repeated that scripture and she passed with an "A." Today she uses it and goes back to that same scripture many times. That scripture has become "rhema" for her.

There are some people in the healing ministry who

maintain that when a scripture strikes you, if you keep repeating it you tend to take it into your spirit. It touches your spirit and will bring healing. "Every Word of God is flawless; he is a shield to those who take refuge in him" (Proverbs 30:5 NIV).

Dr Richard Dobbins, Ph. D., in his book *Your Spiritual and Emotional Power*, tells how he used scripture to heal a woman who feared to leave her home. "Learn to create Bible scenes in your mind when you are anxious or afraid. The Word of God is filled with restful, relaxing scenes. Often, calm can be restored to an anxious person through effective use of mental imagery. That's how I was able to help Gail.

"An attractive woman in her late forties, Gail was highly intelligent and a devoted Christian. Yet, she could not drive herself to her sessions when she first began seeing me. She was frightened the moment she left her house and became terrified by the bustling traffic on our expressways. She had to depend on her husband or a friend to drive her to her appointments.

"In getting acquainted with Gail, I discovered she was very imaginative. Most people who are anxious and fearful have active imaginations, but they are focused on the wrong kind of mental images. Wanting her to discover how her imagination could work for her rather than against her, I asked, 'Gail, what are your three favorite Bible scenes?' She listed them: 'The Twenty-third Psalm, the Good Shepherd and the one lost sheep, and Jesus calming the storm on Lake Galilee.'

" 'Good,' I said. 'Now, I want these scenes to minister to you. First I want you to take three deep breaths.' When she had finished her deep-breathing exercises, dropped her shoulders, and closed her eyes, I suggested, 'While your eyes are closed and you are enjoying such a good relaxed feeling, why don't you picture in your mind the one Bible scene you like most. When you have it in focus, tell me which one it is.'

"Gail's first choice was the Twenty-third Psalm. She worked with that scene until she could picture the green pastures, locate the stream, see the surrounding hills, hear the sound of the shepherd's staff and the bleating of the sheep. I also helped her develop her ability to fix her other favorite Bible scenes in her imagination.

"Gail was instructed to take a few moments before leaving the house to recreate one of those scenes in her mind. Then I reminded her that each of them emphasized the reality of Christ's presence with her everywhere she went. By beginning to focus on an awareness of God's presence and assuring herself that she could do all things through Christ (Philippians 4:13), she was able to drive to her sessions after the first five weeks. By that time, she was also able to shop more comfortably." [6]

Using scripture in active imagination as described in Gail's story is one practical tool to heal anxiety. Most of us can develop this method with a little practice. Remember the "rhema" word comes to us in many ways. God wants to speak that word to everyone. It is in being open to that "rhema" word, expecting it and then appropriating it in our lives that we experience healing.

The words of scripture are life-changing and healing!

The Gospel sequence of the Mass begins with the priest saying, "Almighty God, cleanse my heart and my lips that I may worthily proclaim Your Gospel." This is a private prayer of the priest asking for pure motivation of his heart as he proclaims the Gospel, ". . . cleanse my heart . . ." followed immediately by the words ". . . and my lips . . ." reminiscent of Isaiah's call in the Old Testament to serve the Lord. Isaiah said, ". . . for I am a man of unclean lips . . ." (Isaiah 6:5). "Then one of the seraphs flew to me, holding in his hand a live coal which he had taken from the altar with a pair of tongs. With this he touched my mouth and said: 'See now, this has touched your lips, your sin is taken away, your iniquity is purged' " (Isaiah 6:6-7). Thus the priest before proclaiming God's Word in scripture invokes God's healing touch into his heart and upon his lips. The congregation responds by repeating this healing gesture as they, too, ask that the words of the Gospel be burned into their minds, upon their lips and into their hearts, into consciousness, that they, along with the celebrant and concelebrants, may be doers of the Word, not only hearers. "But be doers of the word, and not hearers only, deceiving yourselves" (James 1:22 RSV).

Let us go through an actual Gospel account to better understand the true nature of God's healing power in the Word.

A reading from the Holy Gospel according to Matthew 22:15-21: "Then the Pharisees went away to work out between them how to trap him in what he said. And they sent their disciples to him, together with the Herodians, to say, 'Master, we know that you are an honest man and teach the way of God in an honest way, and that you are not afraid of anyone, because a man's rank means nothing to you. Tell us your opinion, then. Is it permissible to pay taxes to Caesar or not?' But Jesus was aware of their malice and replied, 'You hypocrites! Why do you set this trap for me? Let me see the money you pay the tax with.' They handed him a denarius, and he said, 'Whose head is this? Whose name?' 'Caesar's,' they replied. He then said to them, 'Very well, give back to Caesar what belongs to Caesar — and to God what belongs to God.' This reply took them by surprise, and they left him alone and went away."

This is the Gospel, the Good News of the Lord Jesus Christ.

Praise to You, Lord Jesus Christ.

The Pharisees said to Jesus, "We know you are a truthful man. You court no one's favor, or act out of human respect" (paraphrased). Who is this that the Pharisees are talking about? Who is there upon the face of the earth that does not court human favor? Who does not act out of human respect to some degree? The Herodians, Jesus' enemies, are saying to Jesus, "We know that You are secure, also we know You speak God's Word as You hear it. You speak with authority. We know that You have it all together and are not concerned with what we think of You. You love Yourself, accept Yourself, see Yourself as good. You have tremendous self-love and because You love Yourself, You do not have to court human favor. You do not have to go around getting others to love You by saying nice things about them."

As we reflect on these thoughts, we might ask ourselves: Do we, like Jesus, love ourselves, forgive ourselves and see ourselves as good, as sons and daughters of the Father? It is in loving ourselves that we are able to love others. The more secure you are, like Jesus, the more you can serve others, the more you will be able to stand up to others in a truthful and sincere manner.

The field of psychology is stressing self-love more and more. Of course, Jesus always did call us to love. "You must love your neighbor as yourself" (Mark 12:31). "In the same way, husbands must love their wives as they love their own bodies; for a man to love his wife is for him to love himself" (Ephesians 5:28). Most Christians are not aware of Jesus' call to love themselves, however, remember we cannot love others except to the degree that we love ourselves.

If we do not think we are good enough to love ourselves, how can we believe that others will love us? In contemporary Christian society, this lack of self-love seems to be a big problem. People also have difficulty believing Jesus loves them because most have been formed in a very negative Christianity. In our tender years we were formed to see God as a judge who is waiting for us to do wrong and punish us, rather than seeing Jesus' teachings on love, acceptance and forgiveness.

The Gospel is saying to us that just as Jesus loved Himself — and He preached the Word telling it like it is, regardless of whose fingers got burned — He is calling us to that same love, so that we can proclaim the Gospel and not have to court favor with others.

As we begin to study and understand the Word of God, the scriptures, we are going to become aware of deeper truths, especially of God's love. God loves us unconditionally as we are. We need to become aware, as Jesus did, of this love. Again I quote from Peter van Breeman, S.J.'s beautiful book *As Bread That Is Broken*: "God cannot but love totally — 100%. If we think God is a person who can divide His love, then we are thinking not of God but of ourselves. God is perfectly one, the perfect unity. We have love, but God is love. His love is not an activity. It is His whole self. If we but grasp some idea of this, we understand that God could not possibly give 100% of His love to His Son and then 70% to us. He would not be God if He could do that. When we read the dialogues of Saint Catherine of Siena, we get the impression that God has nothing to do but simply occupy Himself with Catherine. And that is right. The undivided attention of God is with her and with each of us." [7]

To expand upon the Gospel message of Matthew as reflected above, we might consider the following: If you really believe in the God of the Bible, the God who is love (1 John 4:16), what can you believe about yourself?

1. I am OK as I am, not as I was, or might be. I am lovable just as I am, with all my good points, weak points, sins included.

2. God does not insist that I be perfect, but that I give myself to Him as fully as I can right now.

3. Guilty feelings are harmful. God does not want me to feel guilty about things I cannot change because they are over. God does want me to work through the things I can change.

4. I can admit mistakes, problems and weaknesses without loss of self-respect. It is learning from my mistakes and trying to face my problems that really counts.

5. I am worthwhile regardless of what others say or think about me. Even the people I care the most about cannot destroy my importance or dignity as a person.

6. My importance is not based on what I do or achieve in life, but springs from who I am as a person.

7. I am capable of doing something good for others and achieving some measure of success. I grow as I learn how to give and receive.

8. I can change myself if I really want to and I can shape my future by the decisions I make for myself today.

9. I can still be happy even when life does not go my way. I am about as happy as I choose to be.

10. My feelings about certain things or people do not have to determine my actions toward them.

A GOOD PRAYER TO SAY EVERY DAY: "Lord Jesus, I abandon myself to You. In every way I could think of I have tried to manage myself, to make myself what I thought I ought to be. Seemingly I always fail. Today I give myself with all my failures up to You. I give You permission to take entire possession of me. Help me be what YOU want me to be."

The Word of the Lord as we hear it and as we respond to it within our hearts can be healing whenever we attend Mass. The prayers, responses, psalms and suggested songs for the Mass focus upon the scripture readings. It is here that we find the thread, the theme, that runs through the entirety of the Mass. All the prayers during the Mass lend themselves to that theme. Listen for it as you attend your next Mass. God is speaking to His people in a powerful way, calling us to receive His healing love each and every time we come into His presence through His Word.

This is the Word of the Lord.
Thanks be to God.

CHAPTER 7

The Homily

"By means of the homily the mysteries of the faith and the guiding principles of the Christian life are expounded from the sacred text during the course of the liturgical year. The homily, therefore, is to be highly esteemed as part of the liturgy itself." [8]

The homily is an essential rite of healing in the Mass. In the above quote from the Vatican Council II Documents, clearly and wisely it is stated that the homily is to be "highly esteemed as part of the liturgy". Through the homilist the message of the Gospel is unfolded and explained for the congregation. The homily is meant to complement sacred scripture and further impress into hearts and minds the good news of our Lord Jesus Christ which brings healing. As the theme of the sacred readings are developed through the homily, the ideal would be that the congregation would enter into an attitude of responding to what is being spoken. It is a time of listening for that one word, thought, practical suggestion, inspiration or challenge that will help us to live out our Christianity. Many times it is in listening to a homilist speak that a scripture word heard earlier now becomes "rhema" and one knows with certainty that the

Lord is giving personal direction and guidance. Throughout the Liturgy of the Word the Lord is indeed speaking to His people, calling everyone to become more aware of His presence and love. He is Our God and we are His people.

As the priest begins his homily, it is important to pray silently that the Lord will inspire him. Pray that the words spoken will touch people's hearts and challenge them to live the Gospel of Jesus in a concrete way.

I remember Father DeGrandis stating that many times people shared with him after Mass, "Father, during the homily I heard you say . . . and that was just what I needed to hear." A little surprised, he would reply, "I do not recall saying that." In many cases the average priest does not remember saying what the people have heard. The Lord will sometimes anoint the people and they hear what the Lord wants them to hear. Also the Lord will anoint the priest to speak the words He would have him to speak. Both are anointed because the Church is a sacred place where the power of the anointed word brings healing.

A mother shared with me the story of her son in his twenties who recently returned to the sacraments and Sunday Mass after being away from both for some time. As he started attending Sunday Mass, he shared with her how meaningful the homily was. Week after week the homily became the words he needed to hear. He was amazed how the priest consistently spoke upon some aspect of his life which needed guidance. This young man's mind and heart were open to receive God's Word. As he listened weekly for that word the Lord provided for him, through the homilist, the words directing his daily Christian walk. This shows us that the Lord will speak to us where we are in our lives — through our struggles, our trials, our joys — if we expect and are open to receive.

Keeping in mind that the homily can be healing, what can I expect, as a lay person, from the homily? The following are practical suggestions for listening to a homily.

Expect

"Yes, as the rain and the snow come down from the heavens and do not return without watering the earth, making it yield and giving growth to provide seed for the sower and bread for the eating, so the word that goes from my mouth does not return to me empty, without carrying out my will and succeeding in what it was sent to do" (Isaiah 55:10-11).

"Give ear and come to me; hear me, that your soul may live" (Isaiah 55:2 NIV).

The words of the Gospel are living words and are meant to bring life to all who hear. Even before the homily begins, you can affirm your expectations that God will speak life-giving words to you. "Lord, I expect and believe that You will speak to me through the homilist, that the words I hear will penetrate my mind and sink into my heart. I believe that those words will help me to develop new attitudes which will bring healing and new life."

In listening to the homily, ask yourself the question:

What is God saying to me at this time in my life? For today, this week, what is it I need to hear? Listening is expecting. Listen and expect that the priest will challenge, confirm, inspire, explain, and bring healing to you through the words of the homily.

Throughout the Acts of the Apostles in the New Testament, we can see the early Christians' witness of hope and expectation in the Lord Jesus. They lived in the belief that the Lord Jesus was with them, that He was alive (Acts 1:3) and was daily revealing Himself to them. Their expectations were fulfilled as the Lord did work healings and miracles in them and through them. He directed their lives and increased their numbers even as they believed He would.

In the Upper Room on the day of Pentecost there was great expectation! The apostles, disciples and followers of Jesus were gathered as He had directed. "When he had been at table with them, he had told them not to leave Jerusalem, but to wait there for what the Father had promised" (Acts 1:4). There was great expectation on that day because they believed Jesus' words. What was the promise of the Father that was to come? Those gathered did not have to wait very long. On Pentecost Day they received the Holy Spirit, the promise of the Father. "When Pentecost day came around, they had all met in one room, when suddenly they heard what sounded like a powerful wind from heaven, the noise of which filled the entire house in which they were sitting; and something appeared to them that seemed like tongues of fire; these separated and came to rest on the head of each of them. They were all filled with the Holy Spirit, and began to speak foreign languages, as the Spirit gave them the gift of speech" (Acts 2:1-4). The apostles and first Christians lived in the expectation that the Lord would lead them and guide them.

May we live in the same expectation today as we listen to the homilist explain the life-giving words of scripture!

Carry

"Finally, brethren, whatever is true, whatever is honorable, whatever is just, whatever is pure, whatever is lovely, whatever is gracious, if there is any excellence, if there is anything worthy of praise, think about these things. What you have learned and received and heard and seen in me, do; and the God of peace will be with you" (Philippians 4:8-9 RSV).

Remember to carry within your heart and mind the meaning of the Gospel and the homily during the upcoming week. Reflection might be another word we could use with "carry." Reflect on and carry the meaning of the words you have heard. Many times during the Mass a particular idea might capture your thoughts, but at the time it has no special significance. Do not let that idea or thought go. Its meaning will unfold sometime in the future if you carry it in your heart and wait. There are many things we do not understand readily. In the Gospel of Luke, it is stated that Mary kept many things in her heart (Luke 2:19; 2:52). She pondered them as sometimes we are called to do. Carrying God's Word until it becomes manifest is an important way to grow spiritually in faith.

The words of scripture are life-giving. Again and again we need to be reminded of this. Carrying and reflecting upon Jesus' words and His works transmit a newness of life to all who seek Him. Jesus said, "I have come so that they may have life and have it to the full" (John 10:10). Those are not idle words. Jesus meant those words. Trust that Jesus has come to bring us happiness and peace in our lives. Trust that He brings us new life. He renews and refreshes us. Also trust that what we have heard will be as scripture states about God's Word: "the word that goes from my mouth does not return to me empty, without carrying out my will and succeeding in what it was sent to do" (Isaiah 55:2).

Carrying the words of the Gospel renews us as we become united with the heart and mind of Jesus Christ. Reflecting and repeating God's Word will change our thinking and renew our hearts.

Again, let us seek the example of the disciples and apostles. Many times they carried Jesus' words with them, even though they did not understand (Matthew 13:13; 16:9; Mark 4:13; 8:17; John 8:43). However, they never let it go. Later as time went on, the understanding did become evident and they remembered (Luke 24:8; John 2:22; Acts 11:16). Carrying a word we felt was for us is an act of growing in faith. As we carry a message given to us, God's Word becomes, not a fleeting word, but a word which is nourishing and energizing.

Decide

> "But you must do what the word tells you, and not just listen to it and deceive yourselves. To listen to the word and not obey is like looking at your own features in a mirror and then, after a quick look, going off and immediately forgetting what you looked like. But the man who looks steadily at the perfect law of freedom and makes that his habit — not listening and then forgetting, but actively putting it into practice — will be happy in all that he does" (James 1:22-25).

The last point to keep in mind in listening to a homily is to decide our responses. How are we going to act upon the words heard in the homily?

By way of example, perhaps the Gospel reading of the day was on forgiveness and the priest expanded upon that theme. "Forgiveness, again?" Yes, forgiveness. Forgiveness is one of the major themes in scripture that Jesus teaches us. Upon hearing a homily on forgiveness, one might say, "I do not understand who I have to forgive." "I do not have anyone to forgive." "I have forgiven all I need to forgive." (It is not unusual to hear statements such as these.) However, there is a chance there is someone else we need to forgive. Maybe we do need to "carry" the word on forgiveness during the upcoming week, asking the Holy Spirit to lead us into a new area of forgiveness we have never considered. Then as the Spirit reveals, we can make the decision to forgive. Ask yourself the question: "Do I need to forgive someone I have forgotten to forgive?" "Who 'stepped on my toes' last week that needs forgiveness?" "Perhaps there is a relationship in my life that needs forgiveness?" My experience in the healing ministry proves to me there is always the need to forgive.

Acting upon God's Word becomes healing not only for us but for those around us. Think for a moment what it would be like if everyone acted in a positive way upon a personal word heard first in the Gospel and then in the homily. Surely there would be more peace among all as the message of Jesus Christ would be lived.

As we listen, let us "expect" to hear a personal message; let us "carry" that message with us; and let us "decide" to act upon that word. All of these actions will bring us into the healing love of Jesus Christ.

The following is an article written by Father DeGrandis sharing with his brother priests his personal experiences in delivering homilies. In his travels he hears very positive reports from people, as many are really inspired by homilies. However, complaints are also heard that Catholics do not always hear good, inspiring homilies. So two years ago he sat down one afternoon and wrote some points for powerful homilies.

This article appeared in *Priest Magazine*.

Preaching

"Why do you waste your time on Sunday preaching?" The teenage girl stopped me cold in my tracks. Here I was the young priest who was giving the ministry of preaching all I had. This little girl totally disarmed me. I said a few defensive words and beat a hasty retreat. The next few weeks found me mulling over the effectiveness of preaching. Memories of preachers from my boyhood rose up in my mind. Yes, they had made a difference. They did have an impact on my maturing mind. Above all, I remember the value my father put on Sunday sermons. Ever since then I have been firmly convinced of the power that can be present in the Sunday homily.

Father Joseph A. Hughes, writing in the *Homiletic and Pastoral Review*, October 1980 issue says: "Contrary to a common view that homilies are superfluous or useless, members of the laity say they come to the Sunday liturgy for truth, direction and encouragement."

The words of Jesus are as binding today as when they were uttered: "And preach as you go, saying, 'The kingdom of heaven is at hand' " (Matthew 10:7 RSV). Every priest has developed some techniques for preaching. I believe we need to share with one another what has helped us. The following are some guidelines that have proven helpful to me.

PRAY FOR AN HOUR SOMETIME BEFORE GIVING THE SUNDAY SERMON. If we put in prayer time, the Holy Spirit will touch us and the congregation so that our sermon will be more effective. As men of faith, we must believe that. "Ask and you shall receive . . ." (Matthew 7:7).

SPEAK OUT OF PERSONAL EXPERIENCE. Share what the Lord has done in your life and what scripture passages mean to you. People want to know our inner strivings and lights. People are interested in our relationship with the Lord.

USE SCRIPTURE FREQUENTLY. The homily is an explanation of the Sunday scripture, but we bring in other supporting scripture. Today people are reading scripture more and it is important that we use it well and often.

USE STORIES AND ILLUSTRATIONS FROM TV AND NEWSPAPERS. People are tuned into the media and the more we can use familiar illustrations, the more we catch their attention. One priest uses a *Time* magazine cover as a weekly illustration of his sermon. Another used the Sunday paper in the pulpit.

SHARE THE "GOOD NEWS" OF JESUS CHRIST. We live in a depressing world and people need an uplift. "I came that they may have life and have it more abundantly" (John 10:10). Only Jesus can give answers for happiness in this nuclear world. Let us give hope to a depressed nation.

GET LOUD ONCE OR TWICE IN A SERMON. We need to emphasize what we are saying. A preacher once told a Catholic priest, "We preach, you priests lecture!" Enthusiasm is sometimes missing and people need to hear us get a bit excited about the good News of Jesus

Christ.

SPEAK ABOUT PRACTICAL SUBJECTS. Sometimes people say that we are on a different level and are missing the peoples' needs. We must make practical and relevant the important themes of the new Testament: Who is Jesus Christ? Forgiveness. Faith. Prayer. Justice. Self-Acceptance. Love.

BE POSITIVE AND INSPIRE. People change by encountering the Person of Jesus Christ in a real way. The more we can introduce them to the Lord in an inspiring way, the better. Some people complain that they come away depressed since the homilies are negative. We are preaching to set people on fire with the love of Jesus.

PROVIDE FOLLOW-UP MATERIAL. I always try to have a pamphlet, a leaflet or a booklet available so people can continue to absorb the theme of the homily. We should be able to expect that people will read the material given out as they leave Church so they can continue to nourish their minds and hearts. Sometimes we neglect the possibilities of good literature as a follow-up to a homily. We are battling for people's minds. The more exposure they have to Christian literature, the better.

ENCOURAGE READING OF DAILY SCRIPTURE. So many Catholics are being lured from the Church by the emphasis on scripture by other denominations. We need to show Catholics the value of daily reading and meditating on the Word of God. The Popes have encouraged reading the scripture for fifteen minutes a day over the past years, but Catholics have not generally responded.

A sincere word of thanks to Father Hughes for his

survey which shows that Catholics are still sensitive to the Sunday homily. May the Spirit move us as priests to daily prayer and reflection on the New Testament so that we may share the power of the Word with our people.

I believe when priests preach the Word in a powerful way as listed above people will be healed.

"... and he sent them to preach the kingdom of God and to heal" (Luke 9:2 RSV).

CHAPTER 8

The Creed

"We believe in one God, the Father, the Almighty, maker of heaven and earth, of all that is seen and unseen.

"We believe in one Lord, Jesus Christ, the only Son of God, eternally begotten of the Father . . .

"We believe in the Holy Spirit, the Lord, the giver of life, who proceeds from the Father and the Son.

"We believe in one holy Catholic and apostolic Church."

Thus we begin the Creed. Together we make a profession of our faith before the Lord. We believe in one God: Father, Son and Holy Spirit.

The congregation stands during this time as we are making a decision for Jesus Christ in our lives. "We believe in one Lord, Jesus Christ. . . ." Just as evangelists ask people to make a decision to accept Jesus in order to be saved, we, as Catholics, are repeating in the Mass our profession of faith. We are publicly proclaiming that we accept Jesus and His teachings.

People say, "I was never saved (in the Protestant

sense of the word) before I went to a non-Catholic evangelical assembly." Catholics are often saved but need to be reminded and to pay attention to what they are saying. For myself, I was saved (again in the Protestant sense of a deep awareness of Jesus as personal Savior) when I made my first confession at St. Michael's Church in Lowell, Massachussetts, at age seven. I confessed then, the same as most Catholics. We knelt down and said, "Father, forgive me for I have sinned," and then when we made our First Communion we accepted and received Jesus into our heart. Most of us were saved as children, but just like our non-Catholic friends, as time went on, many times we dropped out of fellowship with our church. In high school, perhaps we started bumming around and because of group peer pressure we fell away from the Church. It does not mean we were not saved. As we recall, we were prepared for a year how to confess our sins and why we were doing this. We knew what we were doing then. Catholics especially need to be reminded of their early Christian teachings and beliefs.

The Creed is a summary and renewal of our faith and belief in Jesus Christ and all that He has taught us. In the recent alleged apparitions of Our Lady in Medjugorje, Yugoslavia (since 1981), she has revealed to the children to whom she is appearing that they are to pray every day, especially the Creed. She even told the visionaries, "The best prayer is the Creed." She once stated to the children to tell the people to pray every day seven Our Fathers, seven Hail Marys, seven Glorias, and the Creed once. "This is the minimum, together with the other Christian duties." She revealed to them further, "Some Christians are no longer believers because they do not pray." Her message, through the children, is a call to repentance, prayer and fasting. She further stated, "All prayer is good if one prays with faith." Our Lady's message is one that everyone needs to examine personally. [9] It is during the Mass we can recall her message and remind ourselves of the extreme importance of saying the Creed. (At this time the authenticity of the apparitions in Medjugorge is still under consideration by the Church, however, the messages of Our Lady in Medjugorge are apparently within the valid teachings of the Church. What I have stated here is only a fraction of the message of Medjugorge.)

In Father Joseph McGloin, S.J.'s book *How to Get More Out of the Mass,* he concisely states this about the Creed: "At this point of the Mass, it's as though somebody asked, 'Are you a Christian?' To answer that question we don't just sit there mumbling; we stand and tell the world that we are indeed Christians, and that this is what we believe as followers of Christ. The fact that we stand means we are proud of what we are about to say, and that we accept the message just read in the Gospel and in the homily.

"If we can call the entrance song a kind of 'national anthem' of our faith, and the opening sign of the cross a sort of salute to Christ, then we can call the Profession of Faith our 'pledge of allegiance.' And for any pledge of allegiance, we naturally stand proudly, to let the world know we mean what we say." [10]

In closing this chapter, let us profess together:

We believe in one God, the Father, the Almighty, maker of heaven and earth, of all that is seen and unseen.

We believe in one Lord, Jesus Christ, the only Son of God, eternally begotten of the Father, God from God, Light from Light, true God from true God, begotten — not made, one in Being with the Father. Through Him all things were made. For us men and for our salvation

He came down from heaven: by the power of the Holy Spirit He was born of the Virgin Mary, and became man.

For our sake He was crucified under Pontius Pilate; He suffered, died, and was buried. On the third day He rose again in fulfillment of the scriptures; He ascended into heaven and is seated at the right hand of the Father. He will come again in glory to judge the living and the dead, and His kingdom will have no end.

We believe in the Holy Spirit, the Lord, the giver of life, who proceeds from the Father and the Son. With the Father and Son He is worshiped and glorified. He has spoken through the prophets.

We believe in one holy, Catholic and Apostolic Church. We acknowledge one baptism for the forgiveness of sins. We look for the resurrection of the dead, and the life of the world to come. Amen.

CHAPTER 9

Prayer of the Faithful

"The 'common prayer' or 'prayer of the faithful' is to be restored after the gospel and homily, especially on Sundays and holidays of obligation. By this prayer in which the people are to take part, intercession will be made for holy Church, for the civil authorities, for those oppressed by various needs, for all mankind, and for the salvation of the entire world." [11]

The prayer of the faithful, or general intercessions, is another opportunity to see God's healing love and power at work through the prayers of the people assembled at Mass. Through united prayer there is tremendous power in the Body of Christ. If we believe in our own personal prayers, how much more can we believe in the prayers of hundreds of people? "Left to ourselves, we probably would not have either the concern or the faith and love to pray for the peace of the world and other enormous prayers like that. But when we make our Prayers of Intercession together at Mass, we learn to make such hopes our own and to trust in the faith and love of the whole Church." [12]

In the Vatican II Documents it is stated that the prayer of the faithful should include intercession for "those oppressed by various needs." In keeping with this thought, I believe, that within our prayer of the faithful we need to include those persons in attendance at Mass who are in physical pain. It is good to pray for people all over the world, for the Church and for salvation — those prayers are to be part of the general intercessions made — however, let us include those persons sitting right next to us in the pew who are in need of healing prayer to relieve their physical ailments and/or psychological traumas. When Mother Teresa went to India, she wondered where to begin in such a vast country of 800 million people. She started with the people right around her. Is the Lord calling us also to begin with the people right around us? Again when we lack the faith to believe in our own intercessory prayer, the supportive prayer of those assembled "props" our faith and belief.

One of the roles of parents is to be intercessors for the family. It is during the time of the 'prayer of the faithful' that parents can exercise their role as intercessors for their families and be channels through which God's healing love will flow into their children.

Pray also for your parish priest, your pastor. He is your spiritual father and he affects you and your family profoundly. He affects your parish family as well as your blood family, having an impact on the whole community. As he is supported in his ministry through your prayer and intercession, more people will be touched by the Lord. There are many people who pray for my ministry. Since January 1980 I have surrounded myself with praying people who are a strong wall of intercessors. I had prayer cards printed asking people to commit up to fifteen minutes of weekly prayer for my ministry. As I minister I am aware of the tremendous prayer power coming from these people who support me in this manner.

Let us take to heart St. Paul's exortation on intercessory prayer: "Pray all the time, asking for what you need, praying in the Spirit on every possible occasion. Never get tired of staying awake to pray for all the saints; and pray for me to be given an opportunity to open my mouth and speak without fear and give out the mystery of the gospel of which I am an ambassador in chains; pray that in proclaiming it I may speak as boldly as I ought to" (Ephesians 6:18-20).

In conclusion, intercession is the responsibility of every Christian. We are told in Galations 6:2: "Bear one another's burdens, and so fulfill the law of Christ" (RSV). To "bear" means to lift with the idea of removing. Another translation uses the word "carry" instead of "bear." Therefore, as intercessors, we are agreeing, not only to pray for, but to bear with and help carry the burden of the other until it is removed. Without the grace and power of the Lord and the support of a loving body of people it would be impossible to do this.

LITURGY OF THE EUCHARIST

CHAPTER 10

The Offertory

"At the beginning of the eucharistic liturgy, the bread and wine destined to become the Body and Blood of Christ are brought to the altar. First of all the altar, which is the table of the Lord, is made ready as the central point of the whole eucharistic liturgy.

"Then the gifts are brought up to the altar. It is both meaningful and desirable that the faithful should bring up the bread and wine; the priest or the deacon receive them at some suitable point, and place them on the altar. While doing this the priest says some prescribed prayers. Although nowadays the faithful do not provide from their own homes the bread and wine destined for use in the liturgy as they did in former times, the ritual of carrying them up to the altar is still meaningful and of spiritual value.

"Money and other gifts for the poor or for the Church may be collected from the faithful and carried to the altar. . . ." [13]

As we now focus on the Liturgy of the Eucharist and its healing elements, I want to reemphasize that the earlier part of the Mass, the Liturgy of the Word, was the Lord manifesting Himself as the Word and we received Him in that manner. Through the words of scripture, through the silence of our own reflections, through the formal prayers of the Mass and through the message of the homily, the Lord revealed Himself and His love for us. It is through the Liturgy of the Word that we enter anew into our love relationship with the Lord as we have experienced His love. Then in response to His expression of love for us, we enter into the Liturgy of the Eucharist in which we can offer ourselves. With the sacrifice of Jesus, this is our sacrifice. We give ourselves to the Lord. Anthropology teaches us that men of all races, for all times, have an inborn desire to make a sacrifice to the power they see greater than themselves.

At the Eucharist, it is the sacrifice of Jesus Christ giving Himself totally to the Father. It can also be a time of giving, sacrificing our lives and the totality of our beings to the Lord. "Father, at this time I give myself to You. All that I am, all that I hope to be, all that I ever was, I offer to You. 'Create in me a clean heart, O God and put a new and right spirit within me' " (Psalms 51:10).

The Offertory

Many people believe that the Offertory, which is the beginning of the Liturgy of the Eucharist is only incidental to the rites of the Mass. Not true! There is healing in every part of the Mass. The Offertory procession itself is symbolic of our coming before the Lord, a time of bringing gifts of water, wine and tithes, but more precisely a time of personal rededication to the Lord. In a certain sense we choose Jesus Christ again as Lord and

Savior in offering ourselves to Him. As the bread and wine is brought up to be offered, we give ourselves with these gifts. The money we contribute is also a sign of the gift of our very lives. "Whatever you do, whether in speech or in action, do it in the name of the Lord Jesus" (Corinthians 3:17 NAB).

As we enter into this central part of the Mass, may I suggest that one of the intentions we offer is our broken and distorted self-image. We can bring to the Father the blemished picture that might have been painted of us through the criticism and remarks of others, asking Him for healing in this area. We are seeking the truth of who we really are before the Lord — we are seeking the truth of who we are in the reality of God's unconditional love. It is the Father's love and acceptance we wish to experience during this time, His healing love. "I have loved you with an everlasting love, so I am constant in my affection for you. I build you once more; you shall be rebuilt, virgin of Israel" (Jeremiah 31:3).

Many times we know ourselves only by what has been reflected to us through others, which could be positive, however, in many instances, the messages given may have been negative. If we look into our primary relationships, especially with our mothers and fathers, many times we can see where distorted messages began. We need to remember that our mothers and fathers have done the best they could. However, as a broken people, we cannot, of ourselves, give love to the degree that others, even our families need love. To the degree we have experienced love, we have also learned love, which we are able to share in return. To the degree we have experienced God's unconditional love, we learn love and we love in return. Consider the experience of Jesus' love for us on Calvary and how we are moved to love in return!

If a child has not experienced love through his parents or those who care for him by the time he is five years old, then most of that child's adult life will be a search for love. The primary role of the father is the communication to his children the concept of the male as a loving and affectionate father. The role of mother is to communicate female love and affection to the child. If we find ourselves lacking in love with these primary relationships, we could be lacking in love with other relationships. So we bring and offer to the Lord that part of ourselves that has lacked love, affection, attention, understanding, warmth and security. We seek to fill these voids with Jesus' love.

Through the words of scripture Jesus tells us, "You must love your neighbor as yourself. There is no commandment greater than these" (Mark 12:31). Jesus, in context, was speaking to Jewish people who knew what love was as they lived in extended families. The Jews were a people who lived in tightly knit communities composed of relatives as well as an immediate family. Children could go anywhere in the village to receive love and attention, which engendered within them a healthy self-love. In most instances, this is far from the experience of our Western modern world. It is difficult for us to love our neighbors to the degree we love ourselves because many times our modern culture lacks ways for us to develop healthy self-esteem. Of course, this is not true in all cultures and I would not want to make such a general statement. However, we cannot give what we do not have. If we do not love ourselves, how can we love our neighbors! Healing of our self-image is basic. As we experience healing in that area, we can, without even working at it, love others more, experience their love and experience the love of our Heavenly Father.

Again, as we begin this rite in the Mass, I believe that our self-image is a primary area we might want to offer the Lord. Be open to sacrifice to Him whatever area of our self-image is damaged or distorted. Bring to Him any brokenness for healing. Remember: OUR HEAVENLY FATHER WANTS TO HEAL YOU.

Tithes

This brings us to the collection, the bringing of our tithes to the altar. How may healing occur here, you may ask? Indeed this seems to be a touchy subject for many. How can one address healing through the collection? There is healing even in the collection! ". . . give, and it will be given to you; good measure, pressed down, shaken together, running over, will be put into your lap. For the measure you give will be the measure you give back" (Luke 6:38 RSV). Tithing is a way to be healed of your financial difficulties, worries and fears. Every person I know who tithes, receives a blessing in return. There are many positive aspects of tithing. Many people who tithe maintain that they have seen healing of their financial condition.

When I was co-pastor in a southern city, the pastor addressed the people with this challenge: "Tithe for three months and if it is a financial difficulty for you, we will gladly refund your money." Not one person who accepted the challenge came for a refund after the three-month trial period.

In New Orleans, Louisiana, a woman once said to me, "For twenty-five years my husband and I have been struggling. We have always been in debt. After I heard a sermon on tithing I started to give. At the end of the year, without any change in finances all of our debts were paid for the first time. I don't understand it, but it happened!"

When the collection basket comes, consider it an opportunity for healing. This can be an act of faith and trust. It is not easy to do. You say, "Father DeGrandis, you just don't understand!" You are right. I don't understand your financial situation. From my own experience I can tell you that in this past year I have given away more money than I have ever given away in my whole life, and I have received more money than I have ever received in my whole life. It keeps getting better. I really believe I have a "rich Jewish father in heaven."

Recently I met a man who tithes 20% of his income. He had received so much by tithing 10% that he doubled it to see if the principle still worked. It did. He is so happy that he can give 20% of his pension income to the Lord. He is so blessed!

Once a man asked me for help because he was going bankrupt. I told him to start tithing. He reacted very angrily. I said to him, "If you want financial help, you need to go to business management firms downtown, but if you want a Gospel response, start tithing." He did start tithing and he saved his business.

Scripture states, "Return to me and I will return to you, says Yahweh Sabaoth. You ask, 'How are we to return? Can a man cheat God?' Yet you are cheating me. You ask 'How are we cheating you?' In the matter of tithes and dues. The curse lies on you because you, yes, you the whole nation, are cheating me. Bring the full tithes and dues to the storehouse so that there may be food in my house, and then see if I do not open the floodgates of heaven for you and pour out blessing for you in abundance" (Malachi 3:7-10). I do not maintain tithing as an obligation, but I will say that as we give to the Lord, He is going to give in return. We know that principle works in prayer. We know it also works in fellowship and in healing. The more you pray for other people, the more healing you will receive. However, many have not tried this in their finances.

During the celebration of liturgy we should experience healing in our whole lives; physically, psychologically, spiritually and economically. Let us give willingly and joyfully!

Preparation of the Gifts

"By the mystery of this water and wine we come to share in the divinity of Christ, who humbled himself to share in our humanity."

Before the prayer is said over the wine to be offered, the priest adds drops of water to the wine in the chalice. This gesture is symbolic of our ultimate goal — transformation into Christ. ". . . it is no longer I who live, but Christ who lives in me . . ." (Galatians 2:20 RSV). This is something very real. A practical example of this transformation is seen in certain people as you sense the light of Christ shining through them. You sense this person is walking with the Lord. It is true for us also that more and more we are being possessed by the Spirit of God who shines through us, both as light and power.

Someone told me that as a priest put his hand on a lady's forehead she said, "I can feel the energy coming out of your hand." That is something very real and tangible. It is the light of Christ and the power of Christ which comes through all of us in varying degrees.

On the Mount of Transfiguration, the power of the Spirit burst forth upon Jesus and the apostles fell flat to the ground because the light of the Spirit shining through Him was brighter than the sun. If you read the lives of the saints you will read that from time to time others could see light emanating from them.

When the drops of water go into the chalice to be mingled with the wine, we are reminded that transformation into Christ is our real goal. We become absorbed in Christ as the water is absorbed in the wine. Daily, during Eucharist, as I see the drops of water going into the wine, it is a reminder that day by day, week by week, year by year, I am being transformed into Christ. This work may not be completed when I die, but through some type of process I will experience a closeness of the Lord until perfectly purified, then go directly into glory and see Him face to face.

The drops of water can be a very powerful remembrance that more and more we are becoming yielded to the Lord. Not our will, but Thine be done, yielding ourselves to do what the Lord wants us to do, when He wants us to do it and as He wants it done.

Washing of the Hands

"Lord, wash away all my iniquities: cleanse me from my sins."

As I wash my hands I always say an additional prayer for guilt. I know the Lord forgives sin, but there is the area of guilt. If we can be healed of this heavy burden of guilt we are released to experience love and to give love.

Guilt is heaped upon us in many ways: our own guilt, parents heap guilt upon their children, brothers and sisters heap guilt upon each other, school teachers upon their students, husbands and wives upon each other and children heap guilt upon one another. Before we reach the age of ten or twelve years old, we can be guilt-ridden without realizing it. Even our birth can be clouded with guilt if we were unwanted, not what our parents expected or born with a birth defect. Guilt can take root within us even at an early age and many people carry that guilt for the rest of their lives. Jesus stands in the place of unconditional love and unconditional forgiveness. If Christianity stands for anything, if Jesus stands for anything, it is this unconditional love and forgiveness. When we experience this unconditional love and forgiveness we will be freed from guilt. The story of the prodigal son comes to mind. (Paraphrased) "I squander my fortune and I return to You, Father, and You receive me. If I go out and do it again, if I do the same seventy times, You will forgive me each time I come down the road. Father, You forgive me unconditionally." Our Father loves us that much. He also tells us to love and forgive unconditionally, which is impossible without the grace of God. So in the washing of the hands, I always add, ". . . and cleanse me of my guilt, Lord."

Pray, brethren, that our sacrifice may be acceptable to God, the almighty Father.

May the Lord accept the sacrifice at your hands for the praise and glory of His name for our good, and the good of all His Church.

CHAPTER 11

The Consecration

"Take this, all of you, and eat it: this is my body which will be given up for you.

"Take this, all of you, and drink from it: this is the cup of my blood, the blood of the new and everlasting covenant.

"Do this in memory of me."

The Consecration of the Mass should be seen in light of the Gospel readings from John 14-16. These are some of the most beautiful chapters in the New Testament. We are not only called to service, but consecration. God loves us. "I am going now to prepare a place for you, and after I have gone and prepared you a place, I shall return to take you with me; so that where I am you may be too" (John 14:2-3). ". . . but the Advocate, the Holy Spirit, whom the Father will send in my name, will teach you everything and remind you of all I have said to you" (John 14:26). These are but a few of the consolations Jesus gave to His apostles. It is a prelude to the consecration of bread and wine. As bread and wine are transformed into Jesus' body and blood, there is a spiritual transformation in each person attending.

To quote Father George Maloney, S.J.: "Eucharist:

The peak of all Christian healing, especially in deeper faith, hope and love on a spiritual plane, should be found in our frequent and devout reception of the Holy Eucharist. It is the New Covenant whereby God continually gives His blood for the remission of sins and the life of the world (Hebrews 9:15, 25-28). In this sacrament that, as priests, we bring to others and also receive each day in the Divine Liturgy, we approach God, the consuming fire (Hebrews 12:29), with great expectancy: that all the sins of our past will be wiped away, that the deep roots of sinfulness in us will be replaced with a new surge of God's eternal resurrectional life in us. Like the woman with the hemorrhage in the Gospel story (Luke 8:43-44), we need only touch Jesus and His power will flow into us bringing us new life.

"Of all the sacraments, the Eucharist is the climax because here Jesus Christ, the perfect Image of the Father, gives Himself unto eternal life. Here He conquers in that eternal now of self-immolation on the Cross for love of us individually all sin and death that exist within us. Here we must experience a sharing in His glorious resurrection as His Spirit dissolves in us our lack of love for God and for neighbor." [14]

The use of visualization is very helpful in the transformation process. Some years ago I visited a chapel in Ann Arbor, Michigan. As I knelt down I noticed there was a priest saying Mass. Super-imposed over the priest was the image of Jesus. I could see Him in a very vague outline, in light. So at the Consecration of the Mass, I have found it very helpful to close my eyes and picture Jesus elevating His Body and elevating His Blood. I picture a white light coming from the Body of Christ, the Blood of Christ to my heart, melting it and bringing me into a healed relationship with myself.

As we go through life we will be hurt and these life hurts will thicken themselves upon our hearts like coats of shellac. After a time our hearts become hardened and cold. The Lord wants to melt our hearts that are coated with resentment, bitterness, negativity. He wants to give us hearts of flesh. Through visualization of the white light coming from the Body and Blood of Christ into our hearts this process can begin.

You might say, "Father, that is poetic. Let's get realistic." Dr. Carl Simonton, M.D., wrote a book entitled *Getting Well Again* which outlines his work with terminally ill cancer patients and the use of visualization in their treatment. Through x-rays he shows the patients their cancer. He has them visualize an army of white blood cells overwhelming the cancer cells and destroying them. Then the dead cancer cells are flushed from the body naturally. This is the medical profession, a medical doctor, using visualization. Dr Simonton has a high percentage of cures with terminally ill patients. He also combines with his program meditation, forgiveness and other approaches, but his main approach centers on visualization. Therefore, when I say that during the Consecration we should picture a white light coming from the consecrated host to our heart, melting it of bitterness and resentment, I am not just being poetic, but very realistic in light of Dr. Simonton's work.

A famous writer, William James, once wrote that your willpower alone cannot change you, but it has to be willpower combined with the use of the imagination. Saint Ignatius Loyola taught that when you meditate on the Gospel of Jesus, put yourself into the scene. Picture yourself beneath the cross of Christ. Hear the people screaming. Hear the wind howling. See the dark clouds swirling above. Hear Jesus as He speaks. This is called composition of place in the spiritual exercises of Saint Ignatius. This method involves the use of our imaginations. It is a powerful asset in our walk with the Lord.

In the past when I worked on liturgies for children, instead of preaching to them, I would give them a Gospel scene and ask them to visualize it. After the meditation, many of them would say things that I knew was far beyond their scope of knowledge and I knew the Holy Spirit was working through their imagination.

At the Consecration close your eyes and see that white light coming down touching your heart, melting those areas of hardness, unforgiveness. See yourself being set free, receiving a heart of flesh full of love, forgiveness and acceptance. See yourself as Jesus sees you: a beautiful person, redeemed, washed in His Blood, accepted, fed with His Body and Blood, Mary as mother, Jesus as brother, with the Spirit as our companion and at one with the Body of Christ.

The Consecration of the Mass is healing as Jesus once again becomes present with us in the Eucharist. Let us visualize His presence as healing light coming into our hearts.

CHAPTER 12

Communion Rite — The Lord's Prayer

"Our Father who art in heaven, hallowed be thy name . . ."

The Lord's Prayer is the perfect prayer given to us by Jesus. It is a prayer of relationship. In this chapter we will explore this beautiful prayer with the intention of opening new areas for meditation in order that we may more fully participate in its mystery. Realizing we can never fully reach the depths of its meaning, its healing power, we enter nonetheless with great expectations.

When we come to celebrate the Mass, we bring what we have, what we are becoming. Regular meditation on the Lord's Prayer sharpens our sensitivity to what our Father wants to do for us and what He expects from us. This combined consciousness of who we are as individuals and as a people who have expectant faith and who trust in Him will release the power of the Lord's Prayer when we pray in unity with the body in the context of the Mass.

We approach our Father in the attitude of repentance and humility realizing our poverty of spirit and at the same time we come rejoicing and in gratitude acknowledging that we are sons and daughters, heirs to the kingdom. We are, "A chosen race, a royal priesthood, a holy nation, a people he claims for his own to proclaim the glorious works of the One who called you from darkness into his marvelous light" (1 Peter 2:9 NAB).

As we say the words "Our Father," we say "yes" to an intimate relationship. God, the great "I Am" has chosen to be our Father. He has chosen to create, nurture, teach, heal, provide, protect, discipline and love each one of us. He holds us in the palm of His hand and promises never to leave or forsake us. The same God who dwells in the highest heaven where He is clothed in power and majesty and from where He governs all things, asks us to call Him "Father" and invites us to be in relationship with Him. It is His desire to abide with us, to dwell in us. This invitation is open; the response is ours. For some it is easy to give a position response; for others, especially those who have had a difficult relationship with their earthly father, this may be very hard to do. If this is the case, it is crucial that we work on healing the father relationship. The following may be helpful in accomplishing this:

1. Ask for the grace to be healed of past hurts dealing with the father relationship, for without His grace we can do nothing.

2. Expect that it will be done.

3. Seek prayer from someone knowledgeable in praying for this type of healing.

4. Use Father DeGrandis' forgiveness prayer found in Chapter 3 of this book.

5. Pray for your father whether living or dead. If he is living, pray blessings upon him. Put no conditions on your prayer.

6. Praise God for your father, whether living or dead. It is not necessary for you to have good feelings about

your father in order for you to praise God for him. Praise is based upon decision, not emotion.

7. Search the scriptures and write down all of the verses that speak to you about God the Father's personal love and care.

8. Repeat these scriptures daily and let them become a part of you.

9. Seek spiritual direction.

Gradually you will be able to accept God the Father's love and enter into a mature relationship with the one whose name is hallowed, holy, set apart. Yahweh, the great "I Am" has chosen to be our Father, our Abba, our Daddy.

"Thy kingdom come, Thy will be done on earth as it is in heaven. . . ."

The Father accepts us just as we are. The gift of salvation, His love, His kingdom, is free, won for us by Jesus' death and resurrection. It is ours because of what Jesus did for us. There is nothing we can do to earn it. "It has pleased your Father to give you the kingdom" (Luke 12:32 NAB). However, as we mature in our Christian journey, it becomes clear to us that our primary purpose is to help build that kingdom right where we are. For each of us there is a specific task in accordance with our vocation, but the life of every Christian is an outside witness of the kingdom within. Without pride or self-righteousness our lives evidence the fact that we are "in" the world but not "of" the world. Into a world filled with darkness, hatred, confusion and hurt, we bring light, love, direction, forgiveness and healing. In the midst of our own brokenness, we bring a message of hope — we bring Jesus. It is that hope which enables us to set our face like flint to do the will of the Father. Jesus said,

"Doing the will of him who sent me and bringing his work to completion is my food" (John 4:34). Food is the staff of life. It is essential for survival. As Christians, to do the will of the Father and complete His work is as important to our spiritual well-being as food is to our body. It is our survival. As individuals and as a body we must be in God's will in order to do His work. If we insist on doing "good works" in our own will we bring division and destruction to ourselves and the Body of Christ, the Church.

It is difficult to admit that our good ideas, our plans, are not always the best way. It is a struggle to give up our will, to die to our ego, acknowledge the gifts of others and become obedient servants. To the degree that we are able to do so, however, we will see good fruit . . . life.

Each of us is an important part of the body who has been chosen, appointed and anointed to do His work. It is in taking our rightful place in that body, being in submission to the will of the Father through it and in working for the good of the whole that we receive the grace and gifts to do God's will and bring His work to completion.

"*. . . yet not my will but yours be done*" (Luke 22:42 NAB).

"*Give us this day our daily bread. . . .*"

Let's look at our priorities. We have entered into relation with our Father and have accepted the responsibility to do His will and build the kingdom. Now we are in right order to enter into petition. We ask Him to provide our daily bread, that is, all that we need to sustain life and accomplish the work we are called to do.

God as always supplied the needs of His people,

through ordinary as well as extraordinary means. It is interesting to know that provision is made at the time of the need, in most cases, not way in advance. We need to have faith that He will always supply our daily bread in spite of circumstances, as He did for the Israelites in the desert (Exodus 16-17), as He provided food for Elijah through the widow who fed him with her last bit of flour and oil (1 Kings 17:7-15), as He provided in turn for that widow and her son after she shared what she had, as he fed 5,000 with a few loaves and fishes (Luke 9:10-17), as he multiplied food for Father Rick Thomas and his community on Christmas Day 1972 to feed the poor in Juarez, Mexico *(Miracles in El Paso?* by Rene Laurentin), as He has provided all that I need, and I am sure all that you need on many occasions. Jesus reminds us that "Man does not live on bread alone, but on every word that comes from the mouth of God" (Matthew 4:4 NAB). It is obvious that we need more than the sustenance received from material provision. We need emotional and spiritual support. This, too, is supplied in abundance mainly through the Word in scriptures, through each other and through the Word made flesh, Jesus, whom we have the privilege of receiving in the form of bread and wine at daily Mass.

> *"And forgive us our trespasses as we forgive those who trespass against us. . . ."*

These words in the Lord's Prayer call us to accountability. It does not put conditions on the Father's love for us but places upon us responsibility to love unconditonally as Jesus did. There is no way that we can do this on our own. It is only through grace and the power of the Holy Spirit living in us that we can make a conscious decision to forgive. Forgiveness, then, is done through an act of the will and is not based upon how we feel about the person or situation involved. We cannot begin to love if we cannot forgive. Unforgiveness blocks love; it blocks receiving. If we could but grasp the enormity that forgiveness plays in our lives, we would be ready to forgive instantly. We would not let the sun go down on our anger. We would forgive not only for the sake of God, for the sake of the other, but for our own sake. For it is a proven fact that when we carry unresolved anger and resentment, we literally make ourselves sick both emotionally and physically. When we refuse to forgive, we block the flow of God's forgiveness to us. Peter asked Jesus, "Lord, when my brother wrongs me, how often must I forgive him? Seven times? 'No,' Jesus replied, 'not seven times; but I say seventy times seven times" (Matthew 18:21-22 NAB). Jesus also said, "I tell you that anyone who is angry with his brother will be subject to judgment. Therefore, I tell you if you are offering your gift at the altar and there recall that your brother has anything against you, leave your gift at the altar, go first to be reconciled with your brother and then come and offer your gift" (Matthew 5:22-23 NAB). These scriptures alone should tell us that forgiveness is crucial in the life of a Christian.

If you have trouble forgiving, ask God to help you to be willing to forgive. You may find it helpful to meditate upon the scriptures dealing with the mercy of God, the Passion, the prodigal son. All of these will help you experience the forgiveness and love of the Father for you. Father DeGrandis' book *To Forgive Is Divine* is a good source of meditation also. Know that the Father is waiting always with open arms to forgive and welcome us back. Let us pray that our attitude and stance will be the same as Jesus': "Father, forgive them for they know not what they do."

Forgiveness is healing and there is no place where this is more evident than throughout the Liturgy of the Mass.

"And lead us not into temptation, but deliver us from evil. . . ."

Immediately after Jesus was baptized by John, He was led into the desert to be tempted by the devil. Read Matthew 4:1-11. Satan tempted Jesus just the same way he tempts us. He offers us all the riches of the world and power as well if we but follow him. Jesus knew the battle we would have in this world. He prayed to His Father on behalf of His disciples and all of us. He said, "I do not ask you to take them out of the world but to guard them from the evil one" (John 17:15 NAB). Jesus overcame the temptations in the desert by using the Word of God in scripture and the authority that was His as God's Son. He tells Satan, "Be gone, away with you, get out of here," after which Satan left and the angels ministered to Him (paraphrased Matthew 4:10).

Temptations begin in the mind and are carried out through the senses — that which we see with our eyes, hear with our ears, feel with our hands or taste with our mouth. If we allow the evil thought, the idea, to take root in our mind, it will grow and we will succumb to the temptation. On the other hand, we can nip those thoughts in the bud. We can, like Jesus, use scripture to battle with the flesh and Satan. Look up and write down the scriptures that best combat your most frequent temptation. Commit these scriptures to memory and use them as weapons against the enemy. Our mind, the battleground of temptation, is consequently transformed. In Romans 12:2 NAB, Paul tells us, "Do not conform yourselves to this age but be transformed by the renewal of your mind." In Philippians 4:8-9 NAB, we read, "Your thoughts should be wholly directed to all that is honest, pure, admirable, decent, virtuous or worthy of praise. Live according to what you have learned and accepted, what you have heard me say and seen me do. Then will the God of peace be with you." We replace destructive thought patterns with positive, wholesome thought patterns.

In addition to using the Word of God to battle our temptations, we bring them to the Eucharist. There is tremendous power in the Eucharist to heal. Of course, we also use common sense in not placing ourselves in situations that would contribute to giving way to our temptations.

When a temptation is deeply implanted it may be necessary to get to its root through special prayer for healing, counseling and spiritual direction. Having the support of others, especially in small group situations, is also very helpful.

In any case, we take courage in knowing that overcoming temptations is an ongoing process. Our desire to do so is the most important prerequisite to receive the grace needed to be delivered.

As I stated in the beginning: the Lord's Prayer is a prayer of relationship. It calls us to love, to trust, to responsiblity and accountability. It is the prayer that Jesus gave us. It is a universal prayer. When we pray the Lord's Prayer, either alone, or with others and especially in the context of the Mass, we are mindful that we are united with millions of other members of the Body of Christ throughout the world who pray this prayer every day. Conscious of these facts, we stand before the Father in awe and humility, in praise and thanksgiving, taking our rightful place as sons and daughters. We dare to say and at the same time boldly proclaim:

Our Father who art in heaven,
hallowed be thy name.
Thy kingdom come, Thy will be done
on earth as it is in heaven.
Give us this day our daily bread.
Forgive us our trespasses
as we forgive those who trespass against us
and lead us not into temptation
but deliver us from evil.

**FOR THINE IS THE KINGDOM,
AND THE POWER
AND THE GLORY FOREVER.**

The kingdom, the power and the glory are His. He extends an invitation to all to become a part of what is His. And our response is:
AMEN! SO BE IT!

CHAPTER 13

Communion

"This is the Lamb of God who takes away the sins of the world. Happy are those who are called to his supper.

"Lord, I am not worthy to receive you, but only say the word and I shall be healed."

"The Eucharistic Miracle at Lanciano: In about the year 700, a Basilian monk in Lanciano, Italy, had continuous doubts about the real presence of Christ in the Eucharist. He could not bring himself to believe that at the words of consecration uttered by him over bread and wine, their substances became the Body and Blood of Christ. But being a devout priest he continued to celebrate the sacrament according to the teaching of the Church and begged God to remove the doubt from him.

"One day, as he was offering the Holy Sacrifice, following the words of consecration, the bread literally changed into Flesh and the wine into Blood. At first he was overwhelmed by what he saw. Then, regaining his composure he called the faithful present to come to the altar to see what the Lord had caused to happen.

"The changed substances were not consumed. The bread-turned-Flesh and the wine-turned-Blood, which later coagulated into five irregular globules, were first placed in a precious ivory container. In 1713 they were enshrined in an artistic silver monstrance in which they are preserved even to the present day in the Church of Saint Francis in Lanciano. Many years later, the Church, wanting to ascertain the true nature of the substances, requested modern scientists to examine them and give their verdict. In November of 1970, a team of medical experts was convened to begin the investigation. It was chaired by Professor Odoardo Linoli. At the start of the investigation he was very skeptical of the matter, but by the middle of December he sent his first message to the Director of the Shrine. It was a very brief but dramatic telegram: 'In the beginning was the Word. And the Word was made flesh.'

"On March 4, 1971, the complete report was ready. The analyses verified the following:

"The Flesh is real flesh. The Blood is real blood.

"The Flesh consists of the muscular tissue of the heart (myocardium).

"The Flesh and Blood belong to the human species.

"The Flesh and Blood have the same blood type (AB).

"In the Blood there were found proteins in the same normal proportions (percentage-wise) as are found in the make-up of fresh normal blood.

"In the Blood there were also found these minerals: chlorides, phosphorus, magnesium potassium, sodium and calcium.

"The preservation of the Flesh and Blood, which were left in their natural state for twelve centuries (i.e. without any chemical preservatives) and exposed to the action of atmospheric and biological agents, remains an extraordinary phenomenon.

"It may be said in conclusion that Science, when called to testify, has given a certain and thorough response to the authenticity of the Eucharistic Miracle of Lanciano." [15]

As the miracle of Lanciano states, we are receiving Jesus and we are to focus on His presence. As Eucharist is received, in your mind's eye, see Jesus standing there giving you His Body and Blood. See Jesus, not the priest. I like to see people focusing on Jesus when they receive the Eucharist. So if I don't give you a wink of the eye or a nod of the head when I give you Communion, it is because your focus needs to be on Jesus. Again I don't want to be hard or unfeeling, but I believe this is a very real theological principle: Jesus is the center of the Mass.

As I travel throughout the country I am shocked. As people receive Communion, what do they do afterwards? As they sit down they watch everyone going to Communion. Now in the third grade I learned you are supposed to pray a communion thanksgiving. That is my Catholic background coming out. If you believe this is the Body and Blood of the Lord Jesus Christ, then as far as healing is concerned, receiving Eucharist is the high point. "Say but the word and I shall be healed."

Saint Augustine says, "When you receive Holy Communion you have the healer Himself." Focus on Him as you sit in your pew or seat. I find it difficult to focus on Jesus with my eyes opened, therefore, I close them.

Regarding Communion prayer, recently I found this page from Father M. Basil Pennington's book, *The Eucharist Yesterday and Today*. Father Pennington states: "The quiet time after Communion is very important. Some people complain that there is so much going on at Mass they can't pray anymore. The silent Mass is gone — and it should be. But silence in the Mass shouldn't be.

"Immediately before Communion each is left to his or her own prayer while the celebrant prepares personally for his Communion and receives his Lord. In the Eastern Christian liturgies a veil is drawn at this time before the altar and a candle placed before it. It is a sacred moment which the community embraces in its silence, expecting the moment of its own Communion when the veil will be opened and the priest will come forth with the chalice: 'With the fear of God, with faith and with love, draw near.'

"The importance and significance of each of the moments should be understood by the worshiping community. I think many have difficulty with the silence because it has never been explained to them, how much it is a part of the whole fabric of their communal worship, which must be true worship and prayer coming from the depths of the heart of each participant. The pause after Communion seems in many ways the most important one." [16]

For a silent Communion reflection, besides the praise rising from the silent depths of our hearts, I offer also, as a suggestion, the staircase of life prayer. You may want to try this prayer silently after your next Communion. However, if you want to sit quietly without doing any mental prayer at all, that's fine too. In the staircase of life prayer, we walk up an imaginary staircase with Jesus and Mary, each step of the staircase being a year. Again we utilize visualization with our prayer. Ask Jesus to supply the paternal/male love that we needed and was not received, especially from our primary relationships. (In an earlier chapter I spoke of this.) Ask Mary to supply the maternal/female love we needed and was not received, again, especially in the primary relationships.

The Staircase of Life Prayer

Jesus and Mary, we ask for the gift of visualization,

enabling us to picture ourselves walking with You up this staircase. Heal the hurts and pains of each year. Supply the paternal/male and maternal/female love we needed. Thank You, Lord Jesus.

I see myself being born as a little infant into Your hands. Take me, Jesus and walk me through the first year of life. Jesus, heal, touch and make whole.

Into the second year of life, especially if I was rejected by any other children in my family. Heal the traumas of the second year.

Lord, I see You carrying me through the third year, healing the hurts and pains, filling me with the maternal and paternal love I needed.

Through the fourth year, I thank You, Lord, for healing the hurts, pains, fears, especially those associated with my family.

Take me gently into the fifth year. Touch me, Jesus. Thank You for walking with me through the first five years of my life.

Touch me gently in the sixth year. May I experience healing, peace, joy, love and life because of Your healing touch.

Into the seventh year, heal all the hurts, pains of going to school, a new teacher, strange children, the trauma of studies, fears associated with moving.

Take me into the eighth year. As I see You carrying and walking with me through the eighth year of my life, heal me. Mary, supply a mother's love that was needed at this time, perhaps because my mother was sick or in the hospital, for any deprivation in the eighth year.

Lord, touch me and supply love in the ninth year, especially supply the affection from my father that I needed and did not receive. Supply that need, Lord.

Thank You for the healings in the 10th year of my

life. Lord, heal any anger I had towards my parents. Touch that anger and give to me a sense of security knowing I am loved. Thank You, Lord, for the healing of the first ten years of my life. Take us through the next ten years, the critical years.

In the 11th year, Jesus, I became self-conscious of my appearance. Heal, touch and make whole. Thank You, Jesus.

Thank you for the healing of the 12th year. Set me free from all the fear and guilt, especially sexual guilt of the 12th year. Thank You, Jesus.

Take me into the 13th year, Lord. Heal, touch and make whole. Set me free from the self-consciousness I felt for being a teenager.

Into the 14th year, I picture You and Mary walking up with me. Mary, supply large doses of a mother's love, giving me a sense of being loved, esteemed and valued.

Touch me gently in the 15th year. Lord, give me a sense of security in this year amidst all my insecurities. Thank You, Lord, for the healings of the first fifteen years of my life.

Into the 16th year, Lord. Touch me now in this difficult year.

Touch me and take me gently into the 17th year, especially times when I hated everything about myself. I ask You to touch me and give me a sense of love and acceptance.

Into the 18th, 19th year, heal, touch and make whole. Touch all the traumas of late teenage years, especially in the area of sexual guilt.

Lord Jesus, touch me deeply in that 20th year when I was rejected by people of the opposite sex. Lord, touch me and set me free. Jesus, thank You for touching me in the 20th year and take us through the years of my twenties. Touch the hurts and pains of the twenties which were so intense, pain in interpersonal relationships.

Lord, I see You taking me into the 21st year, supplying my needs.

Into the 22nd year, especially tension associated with marital partners, in-laws, any bitterness and resentment between families. Heal, touch and make whole.

Into the 23rd year, Lord, heal all the traumas of trying to adjust to marriage, all the misunderstandings and anger that come from this adjustment.

Into the 24th, 25th year. Heal us in the 25th year of our lives when we were so frustrated or felt alone because of a serious illness. Just heal, touch and make whole. Set me free and fill me with your Spirit. I thank You, Lord, for touching the first twenty-five years.

Into the 26th year, seeing death, experiencing death of a close relative: grandmother, father, mother, sister, child, friend, neighbor. Heal the traumas of death and set me free from the many fears of death.

To the 27th year, touch me deeply as I adjust to single living.

In the 28th year, set me free. Let Your Spirit flow through me.

In the 29th year, heal all the feelings of rejection, misunderstandings, false accusations. Touch me deeply and heal me.

Fill me with Your Spirit in the 30th year. Thank You, Lord, for the healing of the first thirty years of my life.

Into the thirties: 31st year, 32nd year. Touch and heal me.

Jesus, heal all the anxieties and fears in the 33rd year, all the care and concern about my children, all the anxieties of my work.

Into the 34th year, Lord. Drinking in the family,

touch that area, Lord.

To the 35th year, I thank You for touching the first thirty-five years of my life. Heal the trauma of difficult decisions.

Jesus and Mary, take me into the 36th year of my life. Heal me and touch me. Heal the tensions of the 36th years.

Into the 37th, 38th year, all the fears associated with job losses, financial difficulties, growing older.

Into the 39th, 40th year. Thank You, Lord, for touching the first forty years of my life. Mary, my mother, give me that sense of closeness, warmth and love.

The 41st, 42nd years. Touch us Lord, in these years of turmoil and change.

The 43rd, 44th years, all the traumas of mid-life crisis, children and leaving home, rejection by a spouse.

In the 45th year, Lord, heal the feelings of failure, feelings that I have not achieved professionally. Also the feeling of not having achieved as a Christian, going through temptations of faith. Lord, heal, touch and make whole.

Into the 46th year, traumas of seeing children leave, marital discord.

In the 47th year, anxiety over grandchildren.

In the 48th, 49th year, take us gently over these years.

Into the 50th year. Heal the first fifty years of life, Lord. Set us free and fill us with Your Spirit.

In the 51st year, heal, touch, make whole.

The 52nd, 53rd, 54th and 55th year of life, let Your Spirit move. Touch all those deep fears, fears of death.

Into the 56th year, 57th year, fears of sickness, loneliness.

Into the 58th year, family moving away, loss of marriage partner, heal and touch those traumas, Lord.

In the 59th year, lack of correspondence with my children. Touch that hurt, Lord.

Into the 60th year, touch the first sixty years of my life.

In the 61st year, heal the feeling of being unwanted, not needed, unappreciated, not understood.

Lord Jesus, take me gently into the 62nd, 63rd, 64th year and heal the fear of approaching retirement.

In the 65th year, Lord, heal the trauma of seeing death in my family.

In the 66th, 67th, 68th and 69th year, heal the hurts and pains over wills and property.

Lord Jesus, take me through the years of the seventies, and let Your love flow through me. Thank You, Lord, for the healings of my life. I ask You, Lord, to say but the word and I shall be healed and set free.

This is a very simple meditation, but it is a very powerful one. It is built on the belief that prayer works, believing that if we ask we are going to receive. Sooner or later, sometime or somewhere, we will enter into a deeper sense of God's love for us. Ultimately we will become happier people because we have experienced God's healing through prayer. During Communion let us focus, through silent prayer, on His healing love.

Lord, I am not worthy to receive You but only say the word and I shall be healed.

CHAPTER 14

The Concluding Rite

"The priest greets the people and gives them his blessing. On certain days and particular occasions he may expand this by including a special prayer over the people and a more solemn form of blessing.

"Finally comes the formal dismissal of the people who may now return to their daily lives of good works, praising and blessing God." [17]

In the last blessing, the concluding rite, the priest, through the power of Holy Orders, is sending you forth to witness, love, serve and heal through the power of Confirmation. My sacrament of witnessing and mission is Holy Orders; your sacrament of mission and healing is Confirmation. You are mandated to heal through this sacrament of witness, Confirmation. The following witness of a dentist, Dr. Willie Andrepont in Groves, Texas, shows how powerful the sacraments of Eucharist and Confirmation really are:

"How can we as dentists cope with the real problems of fear, tension and anxiety in the patient? How often does one hear these statements: 'I hate dentists,' along with 'He hurt me, he used a quarter-inch drill on my tooth. I'd rather do anything, just anything than go to the dentist.'

95

"These fears go back to an incident at a young age caused by a painful experience or hearing one vivid tale of a grownup making a big issue out of a dental experience. Either of these will imbed present fear in the mind of young people. There it remains unless the Lord heals them.

"This is why I believe inner healing in dentistry is on the ground floor and has a long way to go because there is so much work to do in this field. I attend daily Mass and ask the Lord Jesus to heal the people of fears, tension, and anxiety surrounding dentistry.

"In my practice each day, I ask Jesus to anoint each person He sends to the office with His blessings, and heal the pain, fear, tension and anxiety of each one. I ask Jesus to use my hands as His hands in healing and comfort, to guide my hands in working on each patient.

"Jesus has healed many people of all types of problems while in the office — like stopping excessive bleeding, healing an abscess of the gum where there was no tooth, healing an abscessed tooth under a bridge, removing pain and swelling after surgical removal of wisdom teeth, or several teeth nerves regenerated, muscles of the jaw loosened. The Lord has healed some of the patients of ulcers, asthmatic pain, muscle pains, tumors have disappeared, feeling returned to numbed toes, in fact, too many to list in this article.

"In giving myself to the Lord along with His dental office and dental patients, I have realized a greater happiness than ever before.

"Many people really believe that the dentist enjoys hurting people while trying to save their teeth from gum disease or when restoring them. This is far from the truth. There is some pain at times, but it is not inflicted on purpose."

The last blessing sends you forth to love and serve people, your family, your friends. The vision of a new renewed Church is achieved when people realize that they are sent forth to pray with others and serve them in any way they can. Renewal begins within the human heart with the realization that the Lord is sending us forth as witnesses, not just with words, but with action. When Christians start praying with others renewal within the Church will increase significantly. The mandate of Jesus is to go forth in His name to become a source of healing.

The Mass is a healing service and each part of the Mass aids in the healing process. All the major elements of the healing ministry are found present in the Mass: prayer, presence of Jesus, praise, forgiveness. When you go to Church, go with expectant faith, go with great faith that the Lord loves you, wants to heal you and wants to use you as an instrument of His healing love. The Eucharist is the place to begin, the central mystery of our faith.

My prayer: "Father, let us not only go forth with words, but with power. May we have a deeper appreciation and understanding of the mystery of the Eucharist, of the Mass, through the reading of this book."

Visualize Jesus standing at the altar. See light coming from the hands of Jesus coming right into your heart, touching you right now, healing areas of hurt or need. "Father, I pray that the healing light of Jesus will touch all of us at this time." Believe with me that the healing power emanating from Jesus is touching us, setting us free from guilt, self-doubt, self-hatred, self-condemnation, deep healing of the inner man, restoring to us self-esteem, self-love, self-acceptance. "Thank You, Lord, because we believe it is being done to us according to our faith, supplying to us what we need. Thank You, Father."

The Lord be with you.
And also with you.

May almighty God bless you, the Father,
and the Son, and the Holy Spirit.
The Mass is ended.
Amen.

Go in peace to love and serve the Lord.
Thanks be to God.

Notes

1. Austin Flannery, O.P., general edition, *Vatican Collection*. Volume 1: *Vatican 11, The Conciliar and Post Conciliar Documents*. (Northport, New York: Costello Publishing Company, Inc., 1975) p. 16.

2. Theodore E. Dobson, *Say But the Word*. (Ramsey, New Jersey: Paulist Press, 1984) p. 4.

3. Barbara Shlemon, R.N., *The Healing Power of the Eucharist*. Leaflet from Our Lady of Divine Providence, 702 Bayview Avenue, Clearwater, Florida.

4. Peter G. van Breeman, S.J., *As Bread That Is Broken*. (Denville, New Jersey: Dimension Books, 1974) p. 14.

5. John Trenchard, C.SS.R. and Christopher Gaffney, C.SS.R., *The Mass in Pictures*. (Liguori, Missouri: Liguori Publications, 1978) p. 16.

6. Richard D. Dobbins, Ph.D., *Your Spiritual and Emotional Power*. (Old Tappan, New Jersey: Fleming H. Revell Company, 1982, 1984) p. 70.

7. van Breeman, *As Bread That Is Broken*, p. 14.

8. Flannery, *Vatican Collection*, pp. 17-18.

9. Svetzar Kraljevic, O.F.M., *The Apparitions of Our Lady at Medjugorje 1981-1983: An Historical Account With Interviews*, ed. Michael Scanlan, T.O.R. (Chicago, Illinois: Franciscan Herald Press, 1984), p. 91.

10. Joseph T. McGloin, S.J., *How To Get More Out of the Mass. (Liguori, Missouri: Liguori Publications, 1974)*, pp. 80-81.

11. Flannery, *Vatican Collection*, p. 18.

12. Trenchard and Gaffney, *The Mass in Pictures, p. 25.*

13. Flannery, *Vatican Collection*, pp. 174-175.

14. George A. Maloney, S.J., *Healing the Sick: How Can a Pastor Respond, Part II, Crux*, February 1979.

15. Stefano Manelli, O.F.M. Conv., S.T.D., *Jesus Our Eucharistic Love.* (Our Blessed Lady of Victory Mission, R.R. #2 Box 25, Brookings, S.D.: 1973) p. 125.

16. M. Basil Pennington, *The Eucharist Yesterday and Today.* (New York, New York: Crossroad Publishing Company, 1984) pp. 115-116. Copyright © 1984 by the Cistercian Abbey of Spencer, Inc.